THE CHARACTER OF THE WORD

Recent Titles in
Contributions in Afro-American and African Studies
Series Advisers: John W. Blassingame and Henry Louis Gates, Jr.

More Than Drumming: Essays on African and Afro-Latin American Music and Musicians
Irene V. Jackson, editor

More Than Dancing: Essays on Afro-American Music and Musicians
Irene V. Jackson, editor

Sterling A. Brown: Building the Black Aesthetic Tradition
Joanne V. Gabbin

Amalgamation!: Race, Sex, and Rhetoric in the Nineteenth-Century American Novel
James Kinney

Black Theatre in the 1960s and 1970s: A Historical-Critical Analysis of the Movement
Mance Williams

An Old Creed for the New South: Proslavery Ideology and Historiography, 1865–1918
John David Smith

Wilson Harris and the Modern Tradition: A New Architecture of the World
Sandra E. Drake

Portrait of an Expatriate: William Gardner Smith, Writer
LeRoy S. Hodges, Jr.

Race, Politics, and Culture: Critical Essays on the Radicalism of the 1960s
Adolph Reed, Jr.

The White Press and Black America
Carolyn Martindale

Africa and the West: The Legacies of Empire
Isaac James Mowoe and Richard Bjornson, editors

A Black Elite: A Profile of Graduates of UNCF Colleges
Daniel C. Thompson

"De Lawd": Richard B. Harrison and *The Green Pastures*
Walter C. Daniel

Health Care Issues in Black America: Policies, Problems, and Prospects
Woodrow Jones, Jr., and Mitchell F. Rice, editors

THE CHARACTER OF THE WORD

The Texts of Zora Neale Hurston

Karla F. C. Holloway

CONTRIBUTIONS IN AFRO-AMERICAN AND AFRICAN STUDIES, NUMBER 102

GREENWOOD PRESS
NEW YORK • WESTPORT, CONNECTICUT • LONDON

Library of Congress Cataloging-in-Publication Data

Holloway, Karla F. C., 1949–
The character of the word.

(Contributions in Afro-American and African studies, ISSN 0069–9624 ; no. 102)
Bibliography: p.
Includes index.
1. Hurston, Zora Neale—Criticism and interpretation. 2. Afro-Americans in literature. 3. Black English in literature. 4. Dialect literature, American—History and criticism. 5. Feminism and literature—United States. I. Title. II. Series.
PS35151U789Z72 1987 813′.52 86–19457
ISBN 0–313–25264–5 (lib. bdg. : alk. paper)

Library of Congress Catalog Card Number: 86–19457
ISBN: 0–313–25264–5
ISSN: 0069–9624

First published in 1987

Greenwood Press, Inc.
88 Post Road West
Westport, Connecticut 06881

Printed in the United States of America

The paper used in this book complies with the Permanent Paper Standard issued by the National Information Standards Organization (Z39.48–1984).

10 9 8 7 6 5 4 3 2

Copyright Acknowledgments

The author gratefully acknowledges permission to reprint materials from the following sources: the Collection of American Literature, The Beinecke Rare Book and Manuscript Library, Yale University for materials from the James Weldon Johnson Memorial Collection; Harper & Row, Publishers, Inc. for excerpts from *Their Eyes Were Watching God* by Zora Neale Hurston. Copyright 1937 by Harper & Row, Publishers, Inc. Renewed 1965 by John C. Hurston and Joel Hurston; excerpts from *Jonah's Gourd Vine* by Zora Neale Hurston. Copyright 1934 by Zora Neale Hurston. Renewed 1962 by John C. Hurston; and excerpts from *Moses, Man of the Mountain* by Zora Neale Hurston. Copyright 1939 by Zora Neale Hurston. Renewed 1967 by John C. Hurston; J. M. Dent & Sons Ltd. for excerpts from *Their Eyes Were Watching God* by Zora Neale Hurston and excerpts from *Moses, Man of the Mountain* by Zora Neale Hurston; Gerald Duckworth & Co., Ltd. for excerpts from *Jonah's Gourd Vine* by Zora Neale Hurston.

To Russell, Ayana Tamu and Bem Kayin—for sustaining me.
For my mother—whose loving and careful words framed my own.

Contents

Series Foreword

Zora Neale Hurston is the first writer that our generation of black and feminist critics has brought into the canon, or perhaps I should say "the canons." For Hurston is now a cardinal figure in the Afro-American canon, the Feminist canon, and the canon of American fiction, especially as our readings of her work become increasingly close readings, readings which Hurston's texts delightfully sustain. The curious aspect of the widespread critical attention being shown to Hurston's texts is that so many critics who embrace such a diversity of theoretical approaches seem to find something new at which to marvel in her texts.

Karla Holloway's book is the most sophisticated analysis of Hurston's use of language published to date. Holloway's brilliant analysis of Hurston's use of different linguistic "codes," especially her use of the Afro-American vernacular, fastens upon a most fascinating aspect of Hurston's narrative strategy in *Their Eyes Were Watching God*: simply put, that the language of the *narrator*—that the narrator's level of diction—undergoes a profound shift precisely as Janie (Hurston's protagonist) comes to consciousness of herself as a free and strong woman. To a literary critic, this shift of diction is a brilliant example of "free indirect discourse." Holloway's linguistic approach correctly identifies this phenomenon as a profound example of code switching. And by drawing upon Hurston's own theory of language use—as elaborated upon in her essay "Characteristics of Negro Expression"—Holloway is able to show just how self-conscious Hurston's narrative strategy was.

Holloway's book is subtle, accessible, and lucid. It is a model of scholarship, interpretation, and sensitivity. It is destined to define critical approaches both to Hurston's works and to all other works of Afro-American fiction.

Henry Louis Gates, Jr.

Preface

I finally have a whole manuscript before me, completed except for this preface. And as I reflect on the finished text, there seem to be several reasons that have motivated my writing this book. One of them is so that I can claim for my children a tradition of astronomical metaphors. I tell them what my grandmother told me, to "hitch your wagon to a star," and as I am typing I call them over to read how Zora's mother told her to "jump at the sun and you might at least catch hold to de moon." They ask me, again, "Zora who?"

As I have worked on this manuscript, the "Zora who?" question has come to me from a number of directions. To my colleagues in the English department at Western Michigan University, my answer is something like "a foremother of black feminist thought, the legacy who dared writers like Alice Walker and Toni Morrison to be as wonderful as they are"; to my neighbors, whose offers of coffee and conversation on a midsummer's afternoon must be denied because "I am writing," I say she is a "black novelist whose works only recently have achieved the recognition and stature they deserved forty years ago"; to the woman who cares for my children in ways that constantly show me how mothering is a spiritual gift, I ask her if she remembers reading in the black press about a black woman who was accused of molesting a boy back in the forties. It was a sensational story and one my father remembers reading about in the *Baltimore Afro-American*. She remembers as well. "She didn't do it," I say, "and that's who I'm writing about." She hopes I set the record straight. I sigh and worry about the sense of responsibility she has revitalized in me. I tell my children that I'm writing about a woman who was a Hoodoo priestess and who learned magic spells that could satisfy even their imaginations. They want to know some and try them in the backyard. I give them my worn copy of *Mules and Men* and they're off searching for some herbs that don't look like dandelions. My husband knows that I'm still writing about Zora. My parents are not surprised that I am still writing about Zora, and I, encumbered by all my responses to friends, family and colleagues, am even more aware that there is so much about her to say, so many pieces to fit together, that I may always, in some sense, be writing about Zora.

In this book, I have pieced her together as I have learned about her. There is a significant amount of material here that Zora has said about herself, and then there is the part that has come from my understandings in ways female, literary, linguistic and cultural the enigma that was Zora Neale Hurston. Another reason I wrote this book was to acknowledge and celebrate my own legacy and the women who have shaped my soul: my grandparents Marguerite and Celia, my mothers Ouida and Lillian, and Annie Ruth, my friend Mildred—and my understanding that what they have given me is what black women leave to younger generations of black women. As I have worked on this book, these personal awarenesses have meshed with the first empathetic tug I felt from Hurston's spirit when as a student in graduate school I learned of a black woman novelist who found her identity through the words of her people.

In this book, *The Character of the Word*, *word* means more than linguistic inquiry or literary analysis. In it, I assert that Hurston has chosen to be the embodiment of an African legacy and carry the word, the message, through her fiction. That embodiment, understood by her in an academic and artistic sense as a linguist, anthropologist and novelist, is intimately connected to her black self and woman self. The character of her word then, includes these cultural and biological events, and the final reason that motivated my writing this book was an effort to unite these events. The connection with our pasts through the vehicle of the literary word is a connection that takes us back to the oral word. The primacy of those oral traditions is the legacy Hurston's works have assured us we will all share. It is a gift that we must not only acknowledge, but learn to own.

Henry Louis Gates writes that Zora Neale Hurston's "daughters" acknowledge her influence. "They are a tradition within the tradition," he writes, "voices that are Black and women's."[1] Claudia Tate's interview of Alice Walker includes Walker's view of herself as a writer. Walker was the first contemporary black writer to search for Zora Neale Hurston. She sought not merely a grave, but this woman's place in American literature. Walker's statement reads ancient—certainly older than Walker and wide and deep enough to include the many black women writers who have come before her. I sense Zora saying something very similar.

> Writing is... about living. It's about expanding myself as much as I can and seeing myself in as many roles and situations as possible. Let me put it this way. If I could live as a tree, as a river, as the moon, as the sun, as a star, as the earth, as a rock, I would. Writing permits me to be more than I am. Writing permits me to experience life as any number of strange creations.[2]

This is a book about Zora's trees and rivers, her moons, stars and earth. It is a book about the myths she read in men and rocks. This is a book that explores her words as they become and reflect ourselves, our cultures and our beings.

Chapter 1, "The Community in Her Words," presents an overview of the many influences that have contributed to her fiction. It looks both at her fiction and her life as they reflected a woman writing in an age that did not value its women writers. With references to Robert Hemenway's biography of Hurston, I have concentrated on examining the academic and professional "communities" that were responsible for the particular vision of her literary word. The overview in this chapter establishes a perspective for the communities that were more intimately a part of the construction of her words.

The community of chapter 2, "The Crafting of the Word: Art, Artistry and Artist—Stages of Ownership," includes her family, the traditions within her father's house, the backgrounds of his ministry and the New York friends Hurston made for whom she "constructed" an image that met their needs and hers. Critical to this chapter is the view of Hurston in control of her art and her own image. As she came to an understanding and claimed ownership of the cultural traditions that had shaped her, Hurston's choices in the directing of her academic scholarship and her own perspectives toward the subjects of her scholarship would point her literature toward a display of those same traditions. The coalescence of her sociocultural perspectives and her sociopolitical stance would find *completio* in the forms and structures of her literary words.

In chapter 3, "The Emergent Voice: The Word within Its Texts," I pay particular attention to Hurston's novels, since they comprise the largest body of her work. The chapter reviews the way her novels define a development of texts that "speak themselves" into literary being through the character of their words.

Chapter 4, "The Word Assumes Its Raiment and Other Appropriate Garb," develops the concept of text that identifies its own structures through the view of a controlling word. The narrative voice is the operating method in Hurston's fiction, and this chapter explains Hurston's inversion of this voice to reflect the African concept of *nommo*—the word as creator rather than created. Traditional narrative structures in fiction are contrasted in this chapter with Hurston's narrative techniques. The potency of the word, unleashed by Hurston, creates a narrative voice that speaks of, through, for and in a metaphysical blending with characters' voices. Hurston accomplishes such structures for her fiction through her intimate knowledge and use of the black dialect and her assertion that the dialect is the poetic vehicle of the soul. This chapter illustrates that assertion.

The textual inquiry in chapter 5 follows the same lines as chapter 4, but presents Hurston's imagery in her words through linguistic, rather than literary, structures. Using the concept of dialect, and the "adorned word" as its central perspective, this chapter, "The Word, Thus Adorned, Bodies Forth Itself," focuses on the effects of adornment, using linguistic theory as its genesis and a structural interpretative mode to achieve its result. My judgment in the two chapters is that when language is specialized with dialect as Hurston's fiction is, then the literary critic should employ the kinds of analysis that knowledge of dialectal structures affords of text. The nature of the word itself, when rendered in dialectal structures, demands a level of interpretation that meets not only literary tests of analysis, but the linguistic investigations of deep-structure indicators of cognitive processes.

In "The Spiritual Legacy in the Word," chapter 6, I suggest that the point-of-origin in Hurston's critical methodology and literary artistry was her research into the black cultures and communities that culminated in her work on Hoodoo in Jamaica, Haiti and the American coastal areas. These journeys into Hoodoo communities established a research pattern that asserts the primacy of the word in translating significant cultural concepts, in invigorating and sustaining the symbology of the motherland, and in establishing the importance of a spiritual "place" for the bodying forth of a culture. In a chronology, chapter 6 should probably have come first, as I have looked at the genesis of Hurston's words. I placed it last because of its imagery—the word must be grounded, first and last, to assure its vitality.

NOTES

1. Henry Louis Gates, Jr., " 'A Negro Way of Saying,' " review of *Dust Tracks on a Road*, by Zora Neale Hurston, *New York Times Book Review*, April 21, 1985.

2. Claudia Tate, *Black Women Writers at Work* (New York: Continuum, 1983), p. 185.

1

The Community in Her Words

> Yet so many of the stories that I write, that we all write, are our mothers' stories. . . . I have absorbed not only the stories themselves, but something of the manner in which she spoke, something of the urgency that involves the knowledge that her stories—like her life—must be recorded. . . . She had handed down respect for possibilities—and the will to grasp them. . . . Guided by my heritage of love and beauty and a respect for strength—in search of my mother's garden, I found my own.
>
> —Alice Walker, "In Search of Our Mothers' Gardens"[1]

Ironically, Zora Neale Hurston would be no paradox today. Her expertise as a cultural anthropologist, her skills as a linguist and her literary genius would place her firmly in a supportive sisterhood of black writers and scholars who could nourish those talents with their support and understanding. She would be no enigma. As foremother to a generation of black women writers who have developed their excellence in part because Hurston tackled early on the prejudices and disillusion that often taunts excellence in black women, this writer of the Harlem Renaissance merits the intense admiration and critical acclaim she has finally achieved. That the fame comes after her death and that her death was at least in part due to the stress that grew out of an effort to maintain a profession and stature that were eventually cut away from her is testimony to the tragic price black women pay when they cross boundaries that are marked "male" and "white."

Much of Zora Neale Hurston's background reflects her early training and interest in sociolinguistics. Her tutelage under Dr. Franz Boas of Columbia University between 1925 and 1927 developed so intimate an academic relationship that she referred to him as "Papa Franz." It was Boas who arranged the Rosenwald Fellowship in 1935 for Hurston to study for a Ph.D. in anthropology and folklore at Columbia. It was also Boas who underscored the first paradox Hurston was to confront. He taught her the objective skills of cultural anthropology and then encouraged her to think of her people (and herself) as subject for the applications of those skills.

Hurston was a member of the American Folklore Society, for which she published a document on Negro folklore and voodoo practices.[2] She belonged to the American Anthropological Society at a time when this organization paraded the important role of descriptive linguistics in field study. These memberships, as well as her training under Dr. Boas, familiarized her with the then-current attitudes of linguistic investigation. Although these attitudes in one sense stressed cultural relativism and the value of cultural differences, they were fringed with a "noble savage" mind set. Those who studied cultures still felt themselves superior to those cultures studied. It was a unique field for a black woman to invest her talents in. It is not unfair to see "Papa Franz" as the paternal white overseer to this black woman student who called herself Barnard's "sacred Black cow" in a forthright and unambiguous acknowledgment of her status.

Boas, as a descendant of the neogrammarians, began a new tradition in American linguistics by his innovative approaches to language study. He was an anthropologist who believed in the diffusion of anthropology and the unity of cultures—an indication, at least academically, of his belief in the theories of cultural and linguistic relativism.[3] In nineteenth- and early twentieth-century America, the linguistic/anthropological emphasis was on discovering genetic relationships in American Indian languages. Boas's classic 1911 publication of the descriptive view is in his introduction to the *Handbook of American Indian Languages*. According to Boas, field work was the background of significant linguistic investigation. With this orientation shaping Hurston's academic training, it is not surprising that her own field research concentrated on careful documentation of the anthropological/social world of her informants as well as accurate recording of their linguistic usage.

What kinds of sociolinguistic attitudes did Hurston develop from a schooling that encouraged her to examine her own culture and language as an academic curiosity? Her letters, autobiography, short stories and novels provide some clues to her academic philosophy, and her life is evidence of how she survived being thrust so early into the dilemma of being intimately involved in the objective of her scholarly interests. After looking at both, these considerations emerge as basic.

Given her training under Boas, Hurston understood that the language of a people is as important an indication of their culture as are other behavioral manifestations. Further, language is probably a more efficient and accurate means of making a cultural statement than are artifacts, behavior and appearance—traditional cultural markers of anthropological research.

Each of Hurston's novels, as well as her autobiography and short stories, is a careful attempt to record accurately the phonologic, morphological and graphemic characteristics of the dialectal voices in these books and stories. On various occasions she translates vocabulary items and aphorisms that may be unfamiliar to her reading audience.

In her novels, in which characterization is a meticulously constructed event, important patterns emerge. So careful and accurate are these patterns that connect a character's personality, activity and knowledge of self with linguistic activity that it would be a serious error to overlook them or to see them as accidental. They seem, rather, to be Hurston's quite deliberate effort to illustrate the twentieth-century's descriptive-linguistic view in her fiction as it relates to the anthropologists' query. It is because of this pattern, and other patterns that connect language and culture, that speculation concerning Hurston's perspective in the academic and literary arenas is possible.

Because she has, in this age that celebrates black women artists, achieved a fame denied her during her lifetime, Hurston's stature has been recognized by an increasing number of critics and writers.

Robert Hemenway's 1977 biography of Hurston, compiled after his research of Hurston's manuscripts at the Beinecke Library at Yale University and the University of Florida Library and his correspondence with writers of the Harlem school who knew Hurston, is comprehensive. Hemenway constructs a valuable text that blends biographical data and careful literary analysis.[4]

His biography begins at the end of her life, when she writes a letter "in painful longhand" requesting the editors of Harper and Brothers to review her manuscript of *Herod the Great.* From this point, Hemenway flashes back to the earliest parts of her life to investigate what kinds of events would lead a woman who was a prolific writer of novels, folklore and short stories, a graduate of Barnard College, a nationwide speaker whose writings had been praised by national publications and major newspapers, to plead for an unsolicited review of her manuscript from the confines of a welfare home in St. Lucie County, Florida. Hemenway's biography is an absorbing story of Zora Neale Hurston, skillfully combining information from over a hundred different sources and piecing together obscured bits of her life and works until his account of this enigmatic woman begins to fall into place. His research is absolutely thorough and reinforces the critical analysis within his text.

The Hemenway biography, like Lillie Howard's 1980 book on Hurston for the Twayne series, links the events of Hurston's life to her published fiction. Howard concludes her chapter on Hurston's "Life and Times" with a quote from her novel *Their Eyes Were Watching God,* noting that Hurston had "soared to the skies only to fall back to earth. The glory, however, was in the trip itself." Howard then recalls Janie Starks's comment to her friend Phoeby in Hurston's second novel: "If you kin see the light at daybreak, you don't keer if you die at dusk."[5] Both Hemenway and Howard agree that Hurston could not escape her "self" through her writing. Whether it was folktale, drama or fiction, the events of her own life and attitude lie curled between the lines. This cultural and personal mirror is often the result in black art, and Hemenway takes the time to acknowledge this tradition. Fueled not only by the tradition but by an academic preparation that encouraged her to investigate her own background as fodder for anthropological research, it is not surprising that Hurston's footsteps echoed this tradition. Hemenway's discussion of Hurston is a sensitive reflection of her literary contributions. Whether his analysis examines her as woman or black or artist, it is a judicious and careful treatment of a writer who had been too-long-ignored in American letters at the time of his biography.

His stated intent was to present a "new, closer examination of the unusual career of this complex author." In three critical areas: her life, her academic background and her political philosophy, Hemenway's biography is quite successful.

There is not a period in Hurston's life about which Hemenway does not offer some information. This in itself was a remarkable feat because her autobiography was written almost twenty years before her death, and in those twenty years some of the most significant events of her life were to occur. Hemenway is at his best during his discussion of the Harlem Renaissance, a movement that he had written about earlier. Indeed, much of the section of his biography concerning the Renaissance parallels the structure and content of his essay "Zora Neale Hurston and the Eatonville Anthropology."[6] The difference in his biography is that there is more time spent with the critical theories and attitudes of men like W.E.B. Du Bois and Alain Locke, both of whom had a considerable effect on the artistic politics of the Harlem Renaissance. Hemenway carefully traces the influence of Locke, whom Hurston first met while a student at Howard University, and their relationship, which began with his patronage and support and deteriorated into artistic jealousy. In their early relationship he was like her mentor. She actively sought his advice and counsel. The end of their relationship is best documented in an article she wrote for *Opportunity*, which the editors chose not to publish. In this article Hurston lambastes Locke for his inability to appreciate or understand her literary style and the themes that were important to her writing, and she calls her former mentor a "malicious, spiteful snot."[7] Because Hemenway fills in her character and personality, the reader of this biography easily understands the emotional intensity that fueled moments like these in her career and personal relationships.

Toward the end of Hemenway's "Eatonville Anthropology" essay, he speculates that "one reason Zora Neale Hurston was attracted to the scientific conceptualization of her racial experience during the late twenties and early thirties was its *prima facie* offering of a structure for black folklore."[8] He has used his biography to offer evidence to support that early hypothesis. Although Hurston has been dealt with critically, most reference to her, prior to the Hemenway publication, had been as a writer of folktales and four novels. No one sought to make that vital connection between her academic training and the structures of her fiction. Hemenway is aware of the potential for a model that connects the two aspects of Hurston—social scientist and author. He wrote that Hurston "was faced, however, with a scholarly problem: what was her responsibility in explaining her lore? What stance should she take in relation to the folk? How could she make others see this great cultural wealth?"[9] Hemenway suggests that she found these answers within the final formulation of *Mules and Men*. This is true. In *Mules and Men* she was able to blend the scholar and the folklorist in a way that answered the questions Hemenway assumed were her scholarly problems. Hurston was clearly interested in assuring that there would be an audience who could appreciate the culture of her people. The dramatic performances of folk songs, dance and stories that she directed took up a great deal of time during her career and were vitally important to her. She felt that it was one way of allowing her research to do more than decorate some scientific journal. Hemenway underscores this interest in dramatic presentation as being the method she developed for blending art, culture and scientific research. It was, however, an incomplete acknowledgment of Hurston's aesthetic/academic vehicles. Her novels answered as well, if not better, the problems Hemenway notes. Although Hurston did not utilize her fiction in the same obvious way that she used dramas as platforms to present her people and their culture to the world, the fiction became a platform of a more intense, internal and intimate structure. We come to understand her people and her "self" best through the vision of her novels and through the patterns that connect her life and her art with black life and a black aesthetic.

Less critical attention and note have been given to Zora Neale Hurston's politics even though political statement and posturing made up a significant part of the latter part of her life and at least partially account for her fading from the literary scene during these years. Hemenway attempts to circumvent the line of thought that indicates that the 1948 morals scandal involving Hurston's alleged relationships with an adolescent boy was the reason for her literary demise. He quite correctly points out that she did not stop writing after this incident, as some critics had suggested. However, instead of the fiction that characterized the years prior to the incident, she wrote and published nonfiction articles and essays, such as "I Saw Negro Votes Pedaled" and "Why the Negro Won't Buy Communism." The articles had a very specific political intent that Hemenway suggests came from Hurston's attempts "in the late forties and early fifties to transfer her cultural perceptions to the political arena. If she could have found a political outlet for her cultural theories, she might have altered the premises of the American racial dialogue."[10]

Lillie Howard's comment on Hurston's political writings seems to show a more sympathetic understanding of the dilemma Hurston faced after having been born in and having artistically preserved an all-black universe. She notes that Hurston's point-of-reference was the nourishment of her culture and that "negative, self-pitying images of her race" flew in the face of what had nurtured her since birth.[11] Writing the kind of fiction that had given her so much success in her earlier career was perhaps less emotionally fulfilling than her political involvement. Her final project, the massive story of Herod the Great, was an obsession that crowded out other fiction projects for many years. Its rejection, and her pleading from publisher to publisher for a reading of the work is a sorrowful episode to document. Hemenway wrote that the manuscript that Scribner's, David McKay and Harper and Brothers all rejected "suffers from poor characterization, pedantic scholarship and an inconsistent style," noting that the "whole performance touches the heart by revealing a talent in ruins."[12]

The Hemenway biography does much to uncover Hurston's tracks in the years after the publishing of her autobiography. He gives us further insight into this writer in his introduction to the 1984 edition of *Dust Tracks* that includes three chapters her publishers originally extensively revised or deleted from her manuscript. In his introduction to this new edition, Hemenway notes the "image" [that] begs for another dimension" and that the text is "diminished by her refusal to provide a second or third dimension to the flat surfaces of her adult image."[13] Hurston never really fully emerges for Hemenway from the image her one-time employer Fannie Hurst called a "figure in bas-relief." He writes of her zenith years and the destitute years with the same sense of surprise he uses to characterize her use of dialect in her writing. It was a style that failed, he asserts, because it "becomes a kind of camouflage, an escape from articulating the paradoxes of her personality." He sees her autobiography as providing only a one-dimensional view into an image he acknowledges is multifaceted. She remains a paradox for most who seek some reconciliation of the private and public Hurston in the pages of her autobiography or through the reading of her correspondence.

Paul Laurence Dunbar's poem "Antebellum Sermon" is a narrative in dialect that reveals its double entendre in several ways. Most obviously, the preacher in the narrative reminds his audience (knowing the master is likely hiding in the bushes or will be informed by some "loyal" slave) that "Ah'm still a preachin' ancient / Ah ain't talkin' 'bout today."[14] Readers who know the biblical story the preacher's sermon is based on recognize the parallel between the enslaved Hebrew children and the enslaved Africans in America. Most important though, readers who share the dialect, or the heritage of the dialect, recognize that the speech act itself is a way of framing a community, acknowledging a membership and sharing a culture that dissolves the dichotomy Hemenway presents as Hurston. Henry L. Gates, in his review of the most recent edition of *Dust Tracks*, notes how he was "struck by how conscious her choices were. The explicit and the implicit, the background and the foreground, what she states and what she keeps to herself... like a character in her fictions, Hurston wrote herself."[15]

Hurston wrote what is perhaps her most fitting epitaph in her explanation of the theme of *Jonah's Gourd Vine* in a letter to Carl Van Vechten. Her letter to Van Vechten noted that the theme of this novel was "great and sudden growth, one act of malice and it is withered and gone."[16]

Her growth, as a novelist, folklorist and anthropologist, was not great and sudden for her as an individual; but for Hurston as a black novelist, folklorist, anthropologist and black woman the growth was quite sudden. She appeared on the American literary scene without warning, maintained herself there without peer and disappeared from it without notice. The act of malice? Perhaps we can read malice in the almost-passionate insensitivity toward her intent to glorify "her people." Her assertiveness in this regard was characteristic of the black nationalist movement, which had not yet been popularized in black communities when Hurston proclaimed herself "Queen of the Niggerati." It was a position that put her at odds with the majority of the community—scientific, literary and cultural—that she expected would embrace her. Some malice certainly existed in her arrest on the morals charge and her vilification in the black press. The only solace in her prophetic naming of that theme is that she has not withered and gone. Alice Walker assured us of that when she searched Hurston out of an unmarked grave in Florida.[17] Walker's essay "In Search of Zora Neale Hurston" narrates the story of her journey to Hurston's birthplace in Eatonville, and the interviews she had there with folk who knew Hurston. It is a lively sketch of Hurston's personality, especially in her later years, and although it offered no new critical or biographical comment and relied heavily on previously published information, it did successfully return Hurston to the front burners of literary history's acknowledged black voices. Contemporary attention to her searches out all aspects of her contributions and assures us that, unlike the gourd vine, Zora Neale Hurston's roots in American letters are firm.

The attention that Zora Neale Hurston's work received prior to the 1980s revealed the communities that have been influenced by Hurston's artistry. In their writing about Hurston, Ellease Southerland and Mary Helen Washington discuss her in terms that have been important to their own ideologies. Although Southerland identifies her as a novelist/anthropologist, she investigates her work mainly as a novelist and folklorist.[18] Washington's essay on Hurston, in the same edition of *Black World*, is directed toward her women characters as they exemplified the "Black Woman's Search For Identity."[19] This is a common interest in the critical reviews of Hurston's works, and critics have focused on her novel *Their Eyes Were Watching God* as the exemplary indication of this theme. Although only a glimpse of the thematic perspective is explored in Washington's discussion in that journal, Washington has extended her observations in a thoughtful reflection suggesting that Hurston saw herself as a "Woman Half in Shadow" in the introductory essay to Alice Walker's Zora Neale Hurston reader *I Love Myself When I Am Laughing* (1978).[20] Barbara Christian writes that *Eyes* is a "significant novel, a transitional one, in the development of black woman images in literature" and notes that Hurston anticipated "future black women writers who would attempt to define themselves as persons within a specific culture rather than primarily through their relationships with whites."[21] Faith Pullen also notes that the "revolutionary cultural nationalism and feminism of Zora Neale Hurston" was the starting point of much contemporary writing by black women in America.[22]

June Jordan wrote of Hurston's novel of "Black Affirmation" (*Dust Tracks*) in *Black World*. She comments in this essay that "until recently no one had ever heard of her, certainly no one read her books. . . . The fact is, we almost lost Zora to the choose-between games played with Black Art."[23] Prior to the publication of her biography by Robert Hemenway, his detailed and analytical essay in Bontemps's *The Harlem Renaissance Remembered* was the most thorough critical attention she had received.

Even before her discovery in the 1980s, when Zora Neale Hurston was mentioned it was most often in the company of her most popular novel *Their Eyes Were Watching God*. Bone discusses this book in *The Negro Novel in America* and makes this enigmatic appraisal: "the first half of the novel deals with the prose of Janie's life, the latter half deals with its poetry."[24] Although it is this division of style that directs us toward the important discovery of Hurston's linguistic posturing in her fiction, Bone does not use his observation as the basis for further commentary.

It is Jordan's comment about the "games played with Black Art" that identifies the unfortunate conditions surrounding contemporary attention to black artists. In the American readers' "choose-between," Hurston had not been chosen, except to be briefly anthologized or essayed. The recent concern with her is a by-product of the interest in women writers. The critical acclaim of writers like Morrison and Walker has demanded some attention to their heritage. "A generation of splendid writers," writes Henry Gates, "has turned to Hurston for their voices."[25] These writers' acknowledgment of their source stems from their important search for the voice of the foremother, the legacy and image of the ancestor that Toni Morrison celebrates in her works as a necessary presence—"benevolent, instructive, and protective, and they provide a certain kind of wisdom."[26]

We look at writers like Hurston within a black aesthetic because she is mother to a tradition and has given voice to a generation of black women's concerns that may otherwise have been lost. She wrote with contemporaries like Nella Larsen and Jessie Fauset. Larsen's genteel ladies of *Quicksand* and *Passing* find themselves tragically submerged in the intensity provoked by the conflicts of race and color and class. Fauset also deals with the tragic mulatta theme, women who have faith in America and in their light skins so thoroughly that they are immobilized by their delusion. Although Fauset unconsciously illustrated the tragedy of the "color line" that Du Bois promised would be the problem of the twentieth century, Larsen "consciously intensified the pathos and hollowness of the middle-class mulatta heroine image."[27]

Ann Petry, writing in the late forties and early fifties, found some of her best subjects within her own culture. Her 1946 novel, *The Street*, is a sociological study of black motherhood. It is also a novel that sees its stylistic traditions in the naturalistic school and is close to Hurston's *Seraph on the Suwannee* in this respect. Both are stories of women who salvage their selfhood amidst society's unequal afflictions and who are tortured by self-doubt and familial betrayals. Petry went on to greater fame than Hurston was able to achieve, perhaps because she clearly acknowledged that the social battle that was necessary to survive as a black urban woman was different in kind, but not in degree, from the battle to survive the plantation.

This paradox, written about and experienced by Hurston and her contemporaries, made certain that however they lived, and whatever fame they achieved, they would be both the exploited and the exploiter. There were complicated ramifications stemming from the politics of deprivation and racism in America. Writing about those complexities was like doubling their tragic effect.

The development of black literary theory has made it important that the politics and the sociocultural perspectives within this literature be brought together in an intense scrutiny of the text itself, as well as the external forces that have affected its construction. Critical theory has examined this literature in terms of its various pronouncements regarding and documenting black life in America. There is an important body of criticism that explores the many factors that have decided America's social history as reflected in black literature. Such theory has established a firm foundation for the next level of critical inquiry that must emerge for black literature.

Hurston was a mature young woman when she accepted the academic tools of the ethnographer and chose that her literary artistry would be a symbolic tilling of her mother's garden. This was the conscious, thoughtful, careful decision of a woman who did choose, as Gates speculates, to mold and interpret her environment instead of leaving the task to others whom she was sensible enough to mistrust.[28] In her autobiography she wrote that her mother's dying energies so consumed her that "she could not talk. But she looked up at me, or so I felt, to speak for her. She depended on me for voice."[29]

Alice Walker was clearly working bottomland when she acknowledged mothers' gardens—fertile, nurturing, community property of all black women who share the mystery and power of voice. This book is a celebration of that internal voice—the voice of the text and the magic of its word.

NOTES

1. Alice Walker, "In Search of Our Mothers' Gardens," *Ms.* 2, no. 11 (1974), p. 20.

2. Zora Neale Hurston, "Hoodoo in America," *Journal of American Folklore* 44 (October–December 1931), pp. 317–418.

3. C. Dell Hymes, *Language in Culture and Society* (New York: Harper and Row, 1964), p. 115.

4. Robert Hemenway, *Zora Neale Hurston: A Literary Biography* (Urbana: University of Illinois Press, 1977), p. 104.

5. Lillie P. Howard, *Zora Neale Hurston* (Boston: Twayne Publishers, 1980), p. 55.

6. Robert Hemenway, "Zora Heale Hurston and the Eatonville Anthropology," in *The Harlem Renaissance Remembered*, ed. Arna Bontemps (New York: Dodd, Mead, 1972).

7. Zora Neale Hurston, "The Chick With One Hen," James Weldon Johnson Memorial Collection, Beinecke Rare Book and Manuscript Library, Yale University Library.

8. Hemenway in Bontemps, p. 212.

9. Hemenway, p. 159.

10. Ibid., p. 333.

11. Howard, p. 50. Howard's commentary reflects June Jordan's perspective that Hurston's home (Eatonville) was a nourishing and supportive environment because of its blackness and that this early "all-Black universe" was both her literary muse and her base in the "real" world.

12. Hemenway, p. 345.

13. Zora Neale Hurston, *Dust Tracks on a Road* (1942; reprint, Urbana: University of Illinois Press, 1984), pp. xxxvii, xxxix.

14. Paul Laurence Dunbar, "An Ante-Bellum Sermon," in *The Complete Poems of Paul Laurence Dunbar* (New York: Dodd, Mead, 1896, 1913), p. 13.

15. Henry Louis Gates, Jr., " 'A Negro Way of Saying,' " a review of *Dust Tracks on a Road*, by Zora Neale Hurston, *New York Times Book Review*, April 21, 1985.

16. Zora Neale Hurston to Carl Van Vechten, February 28, 1934, James Weldon Johnson Memorial Collection, Beinecke Rare Book and Manuscript Library, Yale University Library.

17. Alice Walker, "In Search of Zora Neale Hurston," *Ms.* 3, no. 9 (March 1975).

18. Ellease Southerland, "Zora Neale Hurston: The Novelist-Anthropologist's Life and Works," *Black World* 23, no. 10 (August 1974), pp. 20–30.

19. Mary Helen Washington, "Black Women Image Makers," *Black World* 23 (August 1974), pp. 10–20.

20. Zora Neale Hurston, in *I Love Myself When I Am Laughing*, ed. Alice Walker (Old Westbury, N.Y.: The Feminist Press, 1979).

21. Barbara Christian, *Black Women Novelists* (Westport, Conn.: Greenwood Press, 1980), pp. 57, 60.

22. Faith Pullen, "Landscapes of Reality: The Fiction of Contemporary Afro-American Women," in *Black Fiction*, ed. A. Robert Lee (New York: Barnes and Noble, 1980), p. 173.

23. June Jordan, "On Richard Wright and Zora Neale Hurston: Notes Toward a Balancing of Love and Hatred," *Black World* 23 (August 1974), pp. 4–10.

24. Robert Bone, *The Negro Novel in America* (New Haven: Yale University Press, 1958), pp. 126–133.

25. Gates, p. 45.

26. Toni Morrison, "Rootedness: The Ancestor as Foundation," in *Black Women Writers*, ed. Mari Evans (New York: Doubleday, 1984), p. 343.

27. Christian, p. 47.

28. Gates, p. 43.

29. Hurston, *Dust Tracks*, p. 87.

2

The Crafting of the Word: Art, Artistry and Artist—Stages of Ownership

> I wish to work out some good nigger themes and show what can be done with our magnificent imagery instead of fooling around with bastard drama that can't be white and is too lacking in self respect to be gorgeously Negro.
>
> —Zora Neale Hurston to Carl Van Vechten, 1927

In her autobiography, *Dust Tracks on a Road*, Hurston's phrases resonate with the poetry of the South's fertile, verdant images and are enriched by the metaphor of her dialect and imagination. With this linguistic background she draws her reader into the series of events that placed her in the mainstream of American novelists and researchers.

Reverend John Hurston, a Baptist minister who was also a landowner and a principal in the governance of the black township of Eatonville, Florida, raised his children in a tradition that embodied a strong religious discipline. The African backgrounds of black American spirituality and worship were essential to this embodiment. Religious celebration within Hurston's fiction reflects imagery representative of an African schema and illustrates not only the experience from her father's house, but the fact that those were experiences rooted in an African sensibility.

John Hurston certainly embodied the preacher Du Bois described as the "most unique personality developed... on American soil. A leader, a politician, an orator, a 'boss,' an intriguer, an idealist."[1] Both the man of her autobiography and the fictionalized father of *Jonah's Gourd Vine* represent this African-American religious man. Du Bois sees this figure as the offshoot of the African priest or medicine man who "early appeared on the plantation and found his function as the healer of the sick, the interpreter of the Unknown, the comforter of the sorrowing, the supernatural avenger of wrong, and the one who rudely but picturesquely expressed the longing, disappointment, and resentment of a stolen and oppressed people."[2] Du Bois further suggests that the earliest forms of Christianity on the plantation were more appropriately "roughly designated" as Voodooism, a link that Hurston herself explored through her research in the communities of Louisiana and the Caribbean.

The discipline that extends from both these backgrounds sets up clearly defined roles for men, women and children within church, family and community. Hurston's was a community that had evolved from the tradition Toni Morrison described in an interview with Eleanor Traylor[3] as an African community during a "time when an artist could be genuinely representative of the tribe and in it; when an artist could have a tribal or racial sensibility and an individual expression of it."[4] This was Zora Neale Hurston—an anachronism of the 1920s—both a foremother and a child not yet conceived. Her community was one that disparaged her, isolated her, viewed her as a curiosity open to public criticism and ridicule and then praised her only to later blame and forget her. This American evolution of the African clan could not support what Morrison describes in that interview as a "public and a private expression going on at the same time." The parallel between Morrison's description of the artist and her relationship to her clan, her community, and Hurston's difficulties as a black woman artist are too compelling to ignore. The community expected a certain role, a specific behavior within accepted patterns. It was the restrictions of these roles that Hurston was to explore in her novels and that led to the personal rebellion that characterized her adult life. Christian writes:

> Unlike most of the other writers of her time, Hurston emphasized the insular folk community as the setting for her works. Although emphatically imperfect, it somehow absorbs the many aspects of its individuals and continually recreates a world view that can sustain them and therefore itself. Hurston was so clearly

> concerned with the peculiar characteristics of the relationship between the black woman and her community that she rarely moved outside it. Perhaps the intensity of her view is related to the position the black woman holds within her community, for she has, since its beginnings, been entrusted with its survival and enrichment.[5]

Hurston's was an ancient spirit in an age that demanded modernism, that called the Negro "new" and expected that Negro to be male.

The unorthodox expressions of her individuality may have been nurtured by her early rebellion within her family, triggered by the death of her mother, and extended as she forced herself into the male networks that adhered to the traditional restrictions of the male collectives of the Harlem literati. Christian's chapter, "An Angle of Seeing Motherhood," in *Black Feminist Criticism* illuminates the paradoxical role of Hurston's girlhood and womanhood that extend from the evolved African-American clan. In the painful description of her mother's death, quoted earlier, which Gates notes as "one of the most moving passages in autobiography," we get a very clear understanding of her link to an African tradition that nurtured the voices and the words of women.[6] Gates contrasts this passage to one from Richard Wright's autobiographical novel *Black Boy*, noting that the death of Wright's mother provoked this response from him: "my mother called me to her bed and told me that she could not endure the pain, and she wanted to die. I held her hand and begged her to be quiet." Here is the essential legacy of Africa—black women carry her voice; their role is to be heard, to distribute knowledge, mother-wit, to vocalize their souls for their children. It is a legacy Hurston was to acknowledge throughout her adult life. Her being gave voice to a generation of black women and left legacies for generations to follow. Wright, through his maleness, calls for silence, and perhaps suggests at least in part the background of some of the hostility Hurston faced from her male contemporaries throughout her professional years.

As an adult, Hurston was both nurtured and stymied by this legacy. She maintained the legacy through her written word—vitalizing black women as self-assertive Janie Starks, questioning the Christian ethic by the pathos surrounding John Pearson and mythologizing the Moses myth so firmly within a black cultural schema that through its color it gained the deepened tones of a folk story. Yet she never actualized, in her personal or literary life, the theme Christian identified as "the primacy of motherhood" that appears frequently in contemporary women's literature as well as that of Hurston's contemporaries, like Nella Larsen, Ann Petry and Jessie Fauset. In Hurston's works, its absence is noticeable. Only in the background of *Seraph on the Suwannee* is there a black family with children, and the children of the white protagonist in this novel suffer exaggerated characterizations. The mother/daughter structures that practically define the black family in Africa and America may have been absent in Hurston's fiction because her adult life lacked a family structure, or because the community she expected would nurture her past the Eatonville days instead hurt and alienated her. After the loss of her mother, Hurston sought a different level in the clan, but her expectations went far beyond what she was to find.

John Mbiti, an African Christian theologian, outlines the critical status of motherhood within African cultures. Descendants validate and enable the persistence of the soul within both the temporal and the spiritual worlds.[7] Hurston felt her mother's call to her for voice, her call to sustain the soul, to assure lineage. Voice for Hurston meant something more metaphysical than physical. It meant acknowledging a potential for motherhood, a role, according to Christian, that was symbolic of contradictions and contrasts.[8] The contradiction came in adulthood for Hurston because she answered her mother's call with spiritual rather than biological allegiance. Her voice was to be heard by a reader rather than passed on to physical progeny, but was still available to any who could participate in the forms of spiritual epiphany that her writing represented. Childless, Hurston was forced outside of the traditional expression of her black femaleness and whether to spite, or in spite of this outsidedness, assumed a lifestyle that exaggerated her isolation.

When a young girl in her father's house, Hurston remembers a scene she describes in her autobiography as twelve "searing stereopticon visions" that etched their way into her mind and permanently affixed themselves to her soul. Her dramatic account of these visions, and their "reenactments" at critical junctures in her life, certainly fit the theatrical mode of this storyteller, and, actual or not, are fitting frames for the telling of her life's story. She insisted that these visions were prophecies of her future and in her autobiography wrote that only after each scene of the visions became a reality did they disappear, one by one, from her waking and sleeping dreams. Through these dreams, Hurston emphasizes the restlessness and disarray of her childhood and the potential her adult life held for sustaining the conflicts of her youth. These scenes gave her a feeling of terrible aloneness. "I stood on a soundless island in a tideless sea," she wrote.[9] Perhaps she looked across the fabric of her fate, already woven by those visions.

Although Hurston remembers her mother's constant exhortation to her children to "Jump at de sun and you at least might catch holt to de moon," it was her father, a physically and emotionally powerful figure in the household, who was a more-frequent image in her writings. It was as if her mother's voice dominated the psychological, and her father's image controlled the visual world of her fiction. Her failed relationships with men, professional as well as personal, may have stemmed both from her mother's death and her father's domination of the family—a domination that made her professional success in a male domain one that took its toll on her personal relationships. In her autobiography, Hurston describes two relationships that failed because she could not find in them the "bright dawn" of love she imagined in her dreams and because she was unable to detach herself from her studies and interests as was "demanded" of her.[10] It seems she accepted these losses in the same spirit that she understood her obligation to choose between intimacy and professional visibility, the public and private expressions of self. But the conflicting voices she used to describe these losses are what is significant. Her first lost is described with a brevity that sustains the image of the alliance itself. The second relationship is described patiently, almost painfully, as its contradictory passions, jealousy, insecurity and selfishness eat away at its heart. Many of Hurston's personal and professional difficulties were indirectly a result of this duality of her professional desires and individual needs. Her failure at reconciliation is the failure of a woman who was at once in control of her talent as well as victim of a system that meted out rewards to those who maintained and supported the male-dictated norms.

The anecdotes of her youth, captured in the first section of her autobiography, are a rich collection of the beacons of her childhood. These intimate accounts of her spiritual growth had to be the very deliberate collection of a woman who understood that she needed to be in control of her professional and public image. She decided to characterize herself as a child who was a dreamer, capturing nature for her personal playmate and directing the moon and stars and the earth in her games. Even in this autobiography it is easy to see how clearly she understands the importance of her allegiance with the natural world. She had portrayed the child Janie in her second novel, *Their Eyes Were Watching God*, with the same connections to nature, finding her developing maturity symbolically imaged in the blossoming of a pear tree.

The reliance on the strength of natural imagery to sustain significance is a distinct characteristic of black American women writers. Toni Morrison writes of using nature as her chorus, a replacement for the choral responses of the clan, in *Tar Baby*. What is important in Hurston's early and definitive role in establishing this tradition is that she records her own growth and maturity with the same natural chorus that is personified in her fiction. It is not merely a fictional tool, it is a cultural truth. Christian writes:

> It is significant, I believe, that Hurston characterizes this relationship [Janie/Tea Cake in *Eyes*] as play, pleasure, sensuality, which is for her the essential nature of nature itself, as symbolized by the image of the pear tree that pervades the novel. . . . Hurston used metaphors derived from nature's play to emphasize the connection between the natural world and the possibilities of a harmonious social order.[11]

I believe she saw her own life as having the potential to reflect that same order, and that many of her sojourns, whether through the New Orleans' Hoodoo community or the Harlem streets, were quests toward finding that connection and establishing its balance in her life. Her almost-fanatical desire to see whatever lay down the dusty road that wound past her father's farm was a desire that was constantly with her in some form—no matter what her vantage point.

Within the tales of a young girl who played better with the boys than with the girls, and whose dolls "caught the devil" from her, is the absorbing recounting of the first time she was visited with her "visions." They began, she wrote, around her seventh year. She recalls: "Soon I was asleep in a strange way. Like clearcut stereopticon slides I saw twelve scenes flash before me. . . . There was no continuity as in an average dream. Just disconnected scene after scene with blank spaces in between. I knew that they were all true, a preview of things to come, and my soul writhed in agony and shrunk away."[12] She surrounds this telling with her familiar use of natural imagery and writes of her precocious understanding of these as images of a future destined to find both fulfillment and heartbreak. They marked her as a child who always "stood apart within." "A cosmic loneliness," she wrote, was her "shadow."[13]

Hurston eventually left her father's house and started down the road that was to exaggerate those feelings of loneliness. Her initial schooling at Morgan Academy and Howard University, the "capstone of Negro education," she wrote, was followed by her enrollment at Barnard College. These two very different experiences, one in black schools that sustained the effects of the supportive black community, the other in a white school that emphasized her isolation from that community, were typical of her experiences and were definitive in nurturing the two voices of Hurston—public and private, subject and object, dialect and standard.

She arrived in New York in January 1925, and shortly after her arrival, established a friendship of sorts with Fannie Hurst. The relationship between the two women began on an employer-employee basis, but Hurston, originally hired as a secretary, grew into a confidante, perhaps racial informant, and friend to Hurst. Hurst writes that she eventually "fired" Hurston because of her lack of ability or interest in the job, but that their relationship sustained itself; although recent biographical information reveals that Hurston moved out of Hurst's home after living there for only a brief month. In a memorial essay to Hurston, Fannie Hurst writes of their meeting:

> She walked into my study one day, carelessly, handsome and light yellow with no show of desire for the position of secretary. We "took a shine" to one another and I engaged her on the spot. What a quaint gesture that proved to be. Her shorthand was short on legibility, her typing hit or miss, her filing a game of find the thimble. Rebuke bounced off of her. "Get rough with me if you want results. I've been kicked around most of my life that your kind of scolding is duck soup to me."[14]

The friends and acquaintances she made in New York were to follow her for the rest of her life—even when she lost contact with them and went into literary and social isolation. In New York she moved in the literary circle that included some of the better-known artists of the Harlem Renaissance and offered a unique contribution to the literature of this age. Her writing signaled a new tradition in black literature as she characterized women like herself, admittedly outside of society, both in terms of culture and gender. She constructed this new image within a literature that was ripe to develop themes like displacement and alienation and outsidedness. The Harlem writers' male enclave was ready to treat these themes racially, and even connect it with a gender—as long as that gender was male; but they were less prepared to see women like Hurston or literary characters like Janie Starks admitting that they were outside of the clan, and surviving it.

The fiction of this age reflected the diverse backgrounds and experiences of many black writers who, like Hurston, had come to New York with little but the promise of being able to practice their craft in the company of others. They took full advantage of white publishers who sought to commercialize the latest fad of America's new leisure class and those patrons who indulged their private fantasies through sponsorship.

The most important relationships Hurston formed during this period were with the Carl Van Vechtens and with Charlotte Mason, the patron that she and other Harlem Renaissance artists called "Godmother." Whatever Godmother's fantasy, Hurston felt that they had a relationship best described as "curious," and she wrote of her conviction that she had been sent to Mrs. Mason to get the key to certain phases of her life. Hurston's autobiography includes a sentimental and now somewhat suspiciously sincere acknowledgment of her indebtedness to Mason, not only for material help, but for "spiritual guidance."

Later perspectives of Hurston's relationship with her sponsor yield the speculation that she was not as dependent on the "spiritual guidance" offered by this "Godmother" as she suggested in *Dust Tracks*. Hughes commented that she felt inhibited by her patrons' restrictions on her lifestyle and that these inhibitions made her nervous and difficult to work with.

Wallace Thurman caricatured Zora Neale Hurston in *Infants of the Spring* as a vampish young woman, Sweetie Mae Carr, taking advantage of the many kinds of assistance available to Negroes who were "in vogue." Thurman suggests that her acceptance of financial assistance and her seeming acceptance of creative guidance were examples of her being out to get all that she could for as long as it was available.[15]

Whether or not it was with gratitude or deception that she accepted the financial rewards of being popular and black, Hurston certainly managed to produce the bulk of her writing during these years and the twenty years following the Renaissance.

The relationship between Hurston, Carl Van Vechten and his wife, Fania, was another liaison that Hurston nourished during her career. The Van Vechtens, too, were sponsors of many black artists, making connections for them with publishers and sponsors and contributing to the success of the Harlem Renaissance years. Carl Van Vechten also contributed to the collection of literature about black America with his highly criticized novel, *Nigger Heaven.* His closest friends, including Hurston and Hughes as well as Fannie Hurst, were quick to come to the artistic defense of this novel. To the larger audience of black middle-class Americans who were uncommitted to the sponsors, their money or their connections, *Nigger Heaven* was clearly an exploitation of the exotic "singularities" of black life in as demeaning and racist a manner as any of the intentionally derogatory tracts that humiliated black America. Sterling Brown commented that the novelist Van Vechten seemed partial to scenes that were selected to prove "Negro primitivism,"[16] but it was Van Vechten's role as friend to the Harlem "niggerati," as Hurston coined the term, that was by far the more important of his contributions to the age.

The letters in the Van Vechten collection at Yale University's Beinecke Library are touching testimonies to the intimate though at times curiously ambivalent relationships maintained among these black artists and the Van Vechtens. Hurston's letters reveal an incredible depth of feeling that extended from her personal and artistic liaison with Van Vechten to her excitement and pride in her professional accomplishments. The letters also reveal her basic insecurities and constant need for encouragement that lay just under the surface of most of her relationships and professional activities. Van Vechten was the recipient of some of her most intimate and sensitive letters in which she abandoned the tough facade and images of her other correspondence.

It was in his role of photographer rather than novelist or confidante that Van Vechten made a more notable contribution to the age. His photographic portraits of Hurston and other Harlem artists poignantly capture the spirit of these writers and are a more worthy testimonial to the age than his attempt at a black literature in *Nigger Heaven.* He took a series of photographs of Hurston around Thanksgiving in 1934. She was in Chicago at the time, and when she got the photos, which show her in moods ranging from smiling to serious to seductive in her fur-trimmed coat and saucy hat, she wrote him a note of appreciation. "Carl," she said, "I am conscious of the honor you do me and feel flattered that you wanted to photograph me." She wrote, "the pictures look swell, I love myself when I am laughing, and then again when I am looking mean and impressive. You are a tall angel with the 'Balsm [*sic*] of gilead' in your hips. I am wearing out my loud singing symbol talking about you."[17] At this early point in their relationship, her letters reflect a certain intensity that makes the tone of their correspondence in her later years that much more credible.

She wrote Van Vechten on almost every important occasion of her life. Her letters reflect the joy and not a little pride at Lippincott's liking *Jonah's Gourd Vine* and *Mules and Men*. One describes her meeting with Langston Hughes in Charleston in August 1927, how "they rolled into this town tonight, tired, but happy." She relates, in characteristic Hurston fashion how, "the back of my skirt got torn away so that my little panties were panting right out in public," and in the same letter discusses her plans for more writing: "I wish to work out some good nigger themes and show what can be done with our magnificent imagery instead of fooling around with bastard drama that can't be white and is too lacking in self respect to be gorgeously Negro."[18]

Her letters also reveal a more honest representation of herself than the recitation of the panty incident intended for the shock effect, or her "good nigger themes" idea, indicating the ambivalence of her distance from her own Negro-ness as well as her claim to it. From her letter of December 1944, "What can I say to put form to my feelings? I have thought and thought. I love you very dearly. If in my struggle with life and the press of the moment I seemed to be indifferent to you, it was less than a mist on the surface of things,"[19] we get a sense of Hurston as a woman maintaining a delicate balance. There is a level of sensitivity here that belies the histrionic image of Hurston that dominates others' memories of her. Van Vechten wrote to Fannie Hurst commending her on a piece she wrote for the *Yale Gazette* commemorating Hurston after her death. He remembers feeling overwhelmed by this woman who was "put together entirely different from the rest of mankind. . . . When she breezed into a room (she never actually entered) tossed a huge straw hat (as big as a cart wheel) on the floor and yelled 'I am the queen of the niggerati,' you knew you were in the presence of an individual of the greatest magnitude."[20]

Although Van Vechten wrote of her as a woman in charge and in control, it now seems that Hurston maintained her public image so carefully that even he did not fully appreciate her depth. The letters between Van Vechten and Hurst, on the occasion of Hurston's death, reveal the misunderstandings and confusion of her friends. Hurst wrote to Van Vechten, "I have often wondered why Zora chose to disconnect herself from our deep interest and friendship."[21]

Her disconnection was, however, not uncharacteristic of a woman who fought so hard to maintain a balance between a public image she sought to define and a private awareness that she belonged more to the world she wrote about in her novels and folk stories than to the world from which she sought recognition and fame. She knew the two were essentially antithetical. In striving to maintain and create a balance, she lived a very fragile existence.

Fannie Hurst wrote that the "inescapable conclusion persists that Zora remains a figure in bas-relief, only partially emerging from her potential into the whole woman. She lived laughingly, raffishly, and at least in the years I knew her, with a blazing zest for life."[22]

Hurst's opinion is characteristic of many who knew Hurston. And Hurston had encouraged this perception of herself, consciously or not, having been forced to decide early in her career to do so. As a "whole woman" ("full-relief"), she was vulnerable and could not fully control the image she knew would determine her fortune. The bas-relief others saw was deliberate. Whether as queen of the niggerati or Sweetie Mae Carr or gorgeously Negro, Hurston was mirror and lamp. She emerged half-cloaked to most of her friends and acquaintances because she knew she depended on them less for friendship than for success—meeting publishers, getting sponsors or maintaining employment. Such friendships were shaky propositions, but Hurston understood the stakes. Henry Louis Gates was also struck with this sense of her duality. When he wrote of the obviousness of her decision to make choices, he detailed her choices as including "the explicit and the implicit, the background and the foreground, what she states and what she keeps to herself."[23]

It is only through the medium of her novels that we begin to glimpse the rest of this woman—author, free spirit, researcher, Hoodoo priestess, black woman and, yes, the title she conferred upon herself, "Zora, Queen of the Niggerati." Her association with Hurst as secretary, companion, and chauffeur and with Van Vechten as friend and confidante are the better-known aspects of her public life. But it was her tutelage under Franz Boas that shaped the research and sociological perspectives that gave her fiction its voices. Under Boas's guidance she became the researcher and anthropologist who trekked through the South, visited the Bahamian Islands, Haiti and South America, and who recorded the folklore and ceremonies of these islands in *Tell My Horse*, determined to show the world what it meant to be "gorgeously Negro."

Hurston's research of Hoodoo gave an insider's view of these mystic practices. In New Orleans, the "sympathetic magicians" initiated her into their community with intricate ceremony. She left Louisiana a full member of that clan, and, thus equipped, headed for a more primary source, the Bahamian Islands. There she collected hundreds of songs, stories and "tunes" that she resolved to make known to the world. In 1932, Hurston introduced the music from these sojourns in a concert at the Harold Golden Theatre in New York City. She undertook the production with a great deal of criticism and very little cooperation from those she had petitioned for help. A letter to Thomas Jones, then president of Fisk University, highlighted the difficulties Hurston experienced.[24]

The initial difficulty she had in arranging the concert was but one minor instance of the personality clashes that proliferated during her career. She was, as Hughes described her, a strong-willed woman who generated conflict and trouble as she tried to impose this will on others. She found it difficult to maintain personal relationships because of her overwhelming sense of self-righteousness and her determination to maintain control of her career. One incident in which this spirit dominated resulted in the breakup of a long and very close relationship with Langston Hughes.

Between 1927 and 1931 Hurston was almost totally involved in research. Mrs. Mason, who had been funding her with two hundred dollars a month for those years, extended her grant through another year and allowed her to collect even more data. Some of this data was eventually used as a thematic base for a play on which she and Hughes had collaborated. The play, "Mule Bone," was never published because of a dispute that grew out of this collaborative authorship.[25] "Mule Bone" is a consummate example of Hurston's deliberate illustrations of how black culture is preserved and illumined through black language and folklore. Her letters to Hughes indicate that she had had enough formal academic training to recognize "some laws in dialect" as well as the dialect's creative capacity to contain the most subtle variation of thought and culture. But their artistic clash over its authorship highlighted her difficulties in maintaining networks, professional or personal, that could see such projects through to their completion. Hurston's social and professional displacement, frequent job shifts, mood swings from happiness to "deep despair" and periods of "grim stagnation" became characteristic of her. Those who knew her best most often discussed her in ways that recognized the existence of these periods of dejection and sorrow.

Her last novel to be published was received with mixed critical response in 1948. It may have been that the subject of the text, which concerned the demise and rejuvenation of a white family's relationships, was too far from her "traditional" subject for her readership, though the book received generally favorable reviews. Lillie Howard's somewhat cryptic comment in her book was that "Zora's readers were in for a surprise. Lo and behold, the woman who had been steeped in, and who had explored the multifariousness of blackness had written a novel about white people." Howard quotes a portion of Hurston's letter to Marjorie Rawlings, with whom she'd developed another friendship that had "paid off." It was Rawlings's introduction of Hurston to her publisher, Scribner's, that resulted in their publication of *Seraph on the Suwannee.* In the letter to Rawlings, Hurston suggested that she was "not so sure that I have done my best, but I tried. I need not tell you that my goal still eludes me. I am in despair because it keeps ever ahead of me."[26] *The Saturday Review* noted:

> Miss Hurston's wonderful ear for the vernacular, for the picturesque phrases and the poetical turn of words that so often is a part of the conversation of the unlettered, makes the novel one that may be read with constant surprise and delight, somewhat aside from its intrinsic merits as a piece of fiction.... All Miss Hurston's fiction has had warmth of feeling—a happy combination of lustiness and tenderness that gives it an appeal too often missing from much of the day's bloodless writing which is sexless in spite of its frequently overwhelming sexiness.[27]

The anniversary of the critical acceptance of this novel is also important for the other anniversary it notes. In September 1948, Hurston was arrested on a morals charge involving an alleged relationship with a young boy in a New York City apartment building. A New York paper quoted portions of the reviews of her latest novel to further sensationalize the story. The review they quoted read: "Miss Hurston shuttles between the sexes, the professions and the races as if she were a man and a woman, scientist and creative writer, white and colored."[28] Her arrest, and the charge of sodomy against her, received headline publicity in the black press. The story was paraded from Baltimore to New York and Chicago. The *Baltimore Afro-American* was one paper that headlined the story and noted that the review of *Seraph on the Suwannee* commented on a character who was "hungry for a knowing and a doing kind of love."[29] That Hurston wrote so poignantly and sharply about intimate relationships proved a liability during this time of trial. Many of the more sensual scenes from *Seraph* were pinpointed throughout the news articles as illustrations of Hurston's own character.

For Hurston, this was a devastating experience. She was "prostrate and hysterical" in the courtroom, defending herself of these charges. She was tried for an alleged relationship with only one youth, not the three in the original charge. Later, both the case and the charges were dropped because of "conflicting and contradictory stories" by the boy involved and the news that the mother of the boy had resented Hurston's advice that the child needed psychiatric counsel. There was also evidence that she had not been in the country when the meetings between her and this child were to have occurred. Fannie Hurst, in a letter to Van Vechten, commented on the incident by saying "the Zora incident—(certainly staged, I understand) is in her fine old tradition. Naughty but nice," and followed the comment with a drawing of a happy, smiling face.[30] Her friends had been so thoroughly deceived by the persona Hurston created for them, the strong-willed, theatrical, joking woman, that they were unable or unwilling to pierce beneath this veneer to comprehend the seriousness and hurt of this incident. The accusations and trial were surely not funny, and the courtroom histrionics of Hurston, who was prostrate with agony, one cannot help but understand as the frightened and angry reactions of a woman accused by the very community she sought to celebrate in her fiction and in her research.

The only absolute certainty is that after this incident Hurston cut off almost all of her communications with her friends and went into a deep, though temporary, depression during which she wrote to Van

Vechten that she would kill herself. She never returned to New York City, and thereafter lived in relative obscurity.

It was in January 1959 that Harper and Brothers received the letter from Hurston asking if they would be interested in "seeing the book I am laboring on at present—a life of Herod the Great." This was, in all likelihood, the same text that she had described with such enthusiasm in a letter to Van Vechten some eleven years earlier. When she wrote Van Vechten then, she had intended for the material to be worked into a play.[31] One year after writing the letter to Harper, Zora Neale Hurston suffered a stroke and died in St. Lucie County, Florida, in the welfare home where she had lived since October 1959. There she was buried, up until the time that Alice Walker "searched" for Hurston, in an unmarked grave. In 1975 Walker left a monument at the Garden of Heavenly Rest in Fort Pierce with the inscription "Zora Neale Hurston, a Genius of the South, 1901–1960, Novelist, Folklorist, Anthropologist." It sits towering over a field of scraggly bushes and weeds that choke the dusty road running past the graveyard.

In Hurston's last years, she had gained weight, fulfilling the prophecy of Fannie Hurst, who wrote of her in that memorial essay that "her lust for life and food go hand in hand." She lost that lust for life, finding her last years as a maid, librarian and sometimes–school teacher a sharp descent from the zenith of her Harlem Renaissance years. Hemenway wrote: "there seems little question that she helped remind the Renaissance—especially its more bourgeois members—of the richness in the racial heritage; she also added new dimensions to the interest in exotic primitivism that was one of the most ambiguous products of the age."[32]

Of the critics who have written about Hurston, Hemenway writes with most clarity regarding the importance of her academic training in her development as a writer. He wrote that she left Barnard in 1927 a "serious social scientist"and observed that her critical and analytical tools gave her the ability to look at her culture both as "subject and object." We forgive and understand her failure and sorrow after her first research expedition following her academic training ended with her crying "huge, salty tears" in front of Papa Franz. This was the first and only attempt she made to erase her culture from her experience, finding her aseptic method of interviewing, "Do you know any stories?", a miserable failure. But the experience did lead her to an eventual understanding of the inadequacy of her "stilted Barnardese" and the critical awareness that her cultural heritage not only held the key to the successful completion of her studies, but the potential for a stellar future built from a positive acknowledgment of her blackness and its utility in an age willing to reward her for being an informant—whether in the linguistic sense or as a novelist/folklorist.

Consequently, her efforts to "construct" a public image that supported her perceptions and that could convey what she felt were the appropriate cultural awarenesses of her race resulted in the bas-relief Hurst noted and the duality noted by her biographer. Perhaps Gates captures best the actual intent of her cloak:

> Hurston, who had few peers as a wordsmith, was often caricatured by black male writers as frivolous, as the fool who "cut the monkey" for voyeurs and pandered to the rich white women who were her patrons. I believe that for protection, she made up significant parts of herself, like a masquerader putting on a disguise for the ball, like a character in her fictions. Hurston wrote herself just as she sought in her works to rewrite the "self" of "the race."[33]

Contrary to what Hemenway suggests as a failure on Hurston's part to find "an expressive instrument, an intellectual formula which could accommodate her varied educational background," Hurston's only professional failure was anticipating that her skills would be fully understood and appreciated on their academic and artistic merits by the community that surrounded her.

I do not believe that her eventual literary silence was compelled by a personal sense of artistic failure; instead, her anger and silence were righteously and accurately directed away from her self and toward those who were unable or unwilling to understand her talent and the academic background of her artistry or to fully accept her within the clan. Although she was quite sure of her excellence, she was less patient with others who, in failing to recognize the worth of her fiction, were denying its subjects as well. This latter situation was untenable for a writer like Hurston, whose purpose was cultural affirmation through the structuring of literary words.

Her attack on Alain Locke, following his review of *Their Eyes Were Watching God*, is an example of her anger at others' shortsightedness. He had criticized the novel as having "contemporary folklore" as its main point, writing that its humor and folklore prevented it from "diving down deep either to the inner psychology of characterization or to sharp analysis of the social background."[34] Hurston was justifiably angry with this shortsighted criticism. Locke's approach to this novel as a book of folklore is obviously flawed and indicates his prejudicial approach to her works. Her passionate attack on his review may be an overreaction, but certainly not out of character for Hurston. The caustic article she wrote for *Opportunity* in response to his review said, "Dr. Locke knows nothing about editing or criticism, would not know a folk tale if he saw one and is abstifically [*sic*] a fraud."[35] The sensitivity of the audience and the artistry of the author were a poor match on this occasion.

Actually, it would have been rather naive of Hurston to feel that her folklore or her fiction would find wide acceptance in the black community; but I do not believe Hurston was naive. Hemenway has suggested that her bitterness over this issue led to her literary demise. I think she must have experienced satisfaction in greater measure over the general critical success her novels earned than over indictments on the level of Locke's. But this was a woman who had sought recognition not only in the eyes of a general public, but who sought membership and respect within the community that had originally nurtured her nationalistic pride. She was fragile in this regard—needing the linkage to the clan that bore her. Her trial was public announcement of her ostracism from a community she sought to celebrate and claim. I believe she could not endure the practical realities of the effects of the trial—the dissolution of her carefully constructed image and the ridiculing of a voice she had tuned to celebrate the beauty of her people. She endured, during that tragic period, a publicity that mentioned her successes, skill and creativity in light of what the public considered to be a woman who had always, in the phrasing of Hughes, "been strange in lots of ways." The carefully forged bas-relief that Hurst noted was the "public" Hurston fell apart in irredeemable style. Her artistry scorned, her womanhood mocked, her professionalism sullied, she wrote to Van Vechten of "the thing too fantastic, too evil, too far from reality for me to conceive . . . I went out of myself."[36] He heard her voice, but, sadly, did not or could not give her in return a spirit he little understood.

NOTES

1. W.E.B. Du Bois, *The Souls of Black Folk* (1903; reprint, New York: Fawcett, 1961), p. 141.

2. Ibid., p. 144.

3. The interview is published as the chapter "Rootedness: The Ancestor as Foundation," in *Black Women Writers*, ed. Mari Evans (New York: Doubleday, 1984). Evans writes, "without Traylor's questions in order to maintain some control over conformity and balance." Traylor is credited with the interview in Evans's preface to the text.

4. Ibid., p. 339.

5. Barbara Christian, *Black Women Novelists* (Westport, Conn.: Greenwood Press, 1980), p. 60.

6. Henry Louis Gates, Jr., " 'A Negro Way of Saying,' " a review of *Dust Tracks on a Road*, by Zora Neale Hurston, *New York Times Book Review*, April 21, 1985.

7. John Mbiti, *The Prayers of African Religion* (Maryknoll, N.Y.: Orbis Books, 1975).

8. Christian, *Black Women Novelists.*

9. Zora Neale Hurston, *Dust Tracks on a Road* (1942; reprint, Urbana: University of Illinois Press, 1984), p. 59.

10. Ibid., pp. 250–260.

11. Christian, *Black Feminist Criticism* (New York: Pergamon Press, 1985), pp. 174–175.

12. Hurston, *Dust Tracks*, p. 57.

13. Ibid., p. 60.

14. Fannie Hurst, "Zora Neale Hurston: A Personality Sketch," *Yale University Library Gazette* 35 (1961), pp. 17–21.

15. Wallace Thurman, *Infants of the Spring* (New York: Macauley, 1925), pp. 229–230.

16. Sterling Brown, *The American Negro: His History and His Literature* (New York: Arno Press, 1969), p. 132.

17. Zora Neale Hurston to Carl Van Vechten, December 10, 1934, James Weldon Johnson Memorial Collection, Beinecke Rare Book and Manuscript Library, Yale University Library.

18. Ibid., 1927.

19. Ibid., 1944.

20. Van Vechten to Hurst, July 5, 1960, Johnson Collection, Yale University Library.

21. Hurst to Van Vechten, Johnson Collection, Yale University Library.

22. Hurst, "Zora Neale Hurston: A Personality Sketch."

23. Gates, p. 43.

24. Hurston to Dr. Thomas E. Jones, October 1934, Johnson Collection, Yale University Library.

25. The file of letters (Johnson Collection, Yale University Library) from Hughes to Van Vechten and from Van Vechten to Samuel French (of Samuel

French Publications) and Hughes details the argument that led to the end of the friendship between Hurston and Langston Hughes. Hughes also mentions this incident in his autobiography.

26. Lillie Howard, *Zora Neale Hurston* (Boston: Twayne Publishers, 1980), pp. 46–47.

27. Herschel Brickell, "A Woman Saved," *The Saturday Review of Literature*, November 6, 1948.

28. "Boys 10 Accuse Zora," *Baltimore Afro-American* 11, October 23, 1948. The news also received the headline "Noted Novelist Denies She 'Abused' 10-Year-Old-Boy" in the *New York Age* 63, no. 23, October 23, 1948.

29. Ibid., p. 1.

30. Fannie Hurst to Van Vechten, Johnson Collection, Yale University Library.

31. Hurston to Van Vechten, 1945 (?). "I am working out something which I hope will be classified as a play. I am using the material around the fall of Jerusalem to Titus in 70 AD. It is a whale of a story, and its greatness lies in the fact that it is universal matter." Johnson Collection, Yale University Library.

32. Robert Hemenway, *Zora Neale Hurston: A Literary Biography* (Urbana: University of Illinois Press, 1977), p. 195.

33. Gates, p. 43.

34. Alaine Locke, "A Retrospective Review (and Biography) of the Literature of the Negro: 1937," *Opportunity* January 1938, p. 10.

35. Hurston, "The Chick With One Hen," Johnson Collection, Yale University Library.

36. Hurston to Van Vechten, October 30, 1948, Johnson Collection, Yale University Library.

3

The Emergent Voice: The Word within Its Texts

> When the writer follows languages which are really spoken, no longer for the sake of picturesqueness, but as essential objects which fully account for the whole content of society, writing takes as the locus of its reflexes the real speech of men. Literature no longer implies pride or escape, it begins to become a lucid act of giving information.
>
> —Roland Barthes, *Writing Degree Zero*[1]

In order to perceive the nature of voice as it emerges through text in Hurston's words, the reader can be instructed by an examination of voice in the four novels. The largest body of her work, the novels, offer a revealing insight. My interpretation suggests that the novels are texts related by a lyrical narrative voice that gains enough strength through its practice and through its involvement in the texts to finally "speak itself" into literary being.

This chapter's discussion may be helpful in illustrating the linkage of voices in Hurston's four novels. Each title reveals that the texts are in a state of creation through their structural relationship to a spirit. *Jonah's Gourd Vine* is a literary allusion to God as a maker and destroyer. "One act of malice," Hurston wrote, and the creative act is "withered and gone." *Their Eyes Were Watching God*, her second novel, forces us into an acknowledgment of that power she signaled in *Jonah*, and the symbolic soul's mirror (eyes) are focused on god—an act that the reader must repeat to discover this book. *Moses, Man of the Mountain* unambiguously propels our vision again, this time upward to a mountain where God resides, and this time the journey is not only spiritual, but Moses is "of" the mountain. The identity implicit in this prepositional structure clearly illustrates that we must physically claim the image to meet the text's challenge. *Seraph on the Suwannee*'s angelic title places someone among the elect. Because we are sure (although Hurston may not have been) by the novel's end that it is not Arvay Henson Meserve, the potential remains open to accept the omniscience such sacred company offers and share in its decision that Arvay does not deserve poetic self-awareness. Instead of embedding these texts into sociocultural critical methodology, which has been accomplished for Hurston's texts amply and well, I have looked for semiological significance in her novels, taking the cue from Ellison who warned us to "consult the text."[2]

In sociocultural criticism, information from outside the text is applied to textual structures, often without careful regard to the text itself. Hurston, in writing three novels about black communities and then one about whites, confounded most of the critics who had developed critical structures that worked only when placed onto the black worlds in her first three novels. The result has been that *Seraph* has been examined very little, and, when studied at all, as an aberration.

Semiology and structuralism are related to the degree that they each compel construction metaphors, building linguistic patterns that reveal man's need to build dependent paradigms when visualizing philosophical concepts.[3] Viewing the significance of the sign as linguistic "act," and, therefore, symbol, and viewing the structures of thought and behavior that pattern those acts as visions are perspectives that extend from the recent schools of Euro-American criticism (Barthes, Lacan, Levi-Strauss, Scholes). This theory organizes a structure of word, act and symbol that acknowledges an ancient view of language. British critic Owen Barfield writes of 'langue' when it was close in nature and degree to 'parole'—when the distance between the speaker and speaker's meanings was not unfathomable, when "poetic, and *apparently* 'metaphorical' values were latent in meaning from the beginning." He writes of myth as an "older, undivided 'meaning' from which poetically disconnected ideas have sprung."[4] Barfield has come closest to defining for these Euro-American schools of criticism what I discuss in this book as *nommo*—the creative potential of the word. My point in highlighting Barfield's perspective here is that, in the face of critical methodology that takes us back to text, Barfield takes the Euro-American critic back to an even more primary source—the word. For Hurston, this source is cultural property as the ancient and complex act of "signifying."[5] The black text that signifies takes its impetus from this linguistic activity and internalizes the process until it speaks to itself. This is the perspective under which I feel Hurston's texts deserve scrutiny because she not only shared the signifying participant-structures with her community, but she worked to enclose those structures into her texts. Because of her acknowledgment of the creative structures in her cultural words, we must look to her texts for the networks that inform them.

Hurston's activation of the word *nommo* to represent the mythology of her culture was probably more a natural act than a self-conscious manipulation of linguistic structures. Hurston's literary talent is unassailable, but what provoked that talent was more closely connected to her belonging to a black community than to her literary inventiveness. It seems to me that in Hurston's texts, structure is what defines theme, and voice is what patterns act. This acquiescence to the primary of the word is acknowledgment of *oracy*—the significant codicil to any definition of black words and black linguistic artful acts. The word, as discussed in this book and other black criticism, has an important connection to the natural world. But the critical inquiry that necessarily accompanies those discussions of black literature and language is that which looks to the nature of black words themselves—a view that is inclusive of the physical world, the spiritual universe and the creative power in the alignment of the two. That is why the black word creates; and as it is discussed as the language of the community the imagery of nature and the symbol of the spirit, we must remember that it is all of these things as well as each of them. I propose a look at Hurston's texts as examples of the word complete as complement to the criticism that explores the novels as the collocation of symbols and events that construct their wholes.

I have noted that *Jonah's Gourd Vine* is a novel that foreshadows its own tragedy through its title. Whose gourd vine? John Pearson, as a mulatto, may not be a man who is "tragically colored" in this novel, but he is doomed through his association with that vine and its empty fruit. The novel gathers its massive strength not from its story, nor from the characters, but from the magical words that cause a congregation to enfold its wayward preacher in its compassion and force him back to a pulpit he has threatened to leave. Hurston had determined in this novel that neither the characters nor the events have power equal to the word. In a pastiche that links this preacher's prayer with James Weldon Johnson's "Listen Lord,"[6] John Pearson finds "a prayin' ground," a place for his words: "O Lawd, heah 'tis once mo and again yo' weak and humble servant is knee-bent and body-bowed—Mah heart beneath mah knees and mah knees in some lonesome valley."[7] In this brief prayer, John fulfills the signal of the novel's title. He draws inward toward salvation; but outside of his soul, his spiritual impotence bears his destruction. He pleads for mercy and that the "ranges uh mah deceitful mind" be plucked out before it condemns him. Self-fulfilling, the novel and the character John structure their own outcome. It is possible, certainly, to reference the African images of his spirituality, and it is valuable to recognize his connection to spiritual men in Africa—but the text itself also pleads for a recognition of its intrinsic structure, one that feeds on its own signs and is transformed by its own linguistic activity.

John is a paradox—saint and sinner. This schism is the underlying conflict of the text, and, from its revelation, calls for the destruction of those involved. The prayers uttered by John Pearson should, by rights, be prayers for others—it is for his congregation that his words are meant. His role, ancient or contemporary, is to give life to the community by the enlivening of their spirits. But John is a contradiction and voice takes on its own power to deflate the effects of his physical impotence. His inability to call for the reconciliation of body and soul means that he will eventually lose control of his prayers' power (the word activated), and the spirit he calls on for salvation will destroy him, as it did that gourd vine, in order to extricate itself from this human strayed too far from the creative, nurturing word. The novel builds its own explosive potential through the series of sermons and prayers that climb to a fever pitch, with John's dishonest manipulation of the word at the center of his destruction. He preaches a sermon wittingly structured to move the congregation to forgive him his sins. But John's petition is wrongfully directed and though the church "surged up, a weeping wave about him" and forgives his transgressions, he is struck with a more serious malady—losing the power of the word he has abused. Hurston pictures him feeling as if he were asleep, losing the power that had been in his voice, saying "nothing . . . his words . . . very few" and his spirit calling through him for the power to flee, "oh for the wings, the wings of a dove."[8] The structure of the text, built on words invested with power wrongfully separated from their human conduits, demands that if this flight is realized, it will split the body from the spirit—a sacrifice exacted to assure that the word is no longer threatened by the dishonest preacher. So John loses his life, frees his spirit and its voice to the air.

Hurston leaves this voice airborne and then brings it back as a wind in *Their Eyes Were Watching God*. Here, all the mighty fury of the word unleashed turns the soul inward and forces an acknowledgment of its strength. Hurston leads us, in a novel complicated in ways that make it nearly impossible to leave this text, to her powerful word. "The winds came back," she wrote, "with a triple fury," in a section where the allusion to the voice of God in the whirlwind is clear. The supporting structures of text that dissemble in the fury of this voice are what make it a book that talks to itself.

Hurston develops her character Janie to the point that she is an assertive, self-fulfilled woman. Weaving her maturity through the natural imagery of the pear tree, through a fertile farmland with Logan Killicks where her spirit is spoiled, and into a town grown out of wilderness tamed, Hurston's word destroys sexual and natural fertility. Her word sweeps through with the force of a hurricane destroying all the structures so carefully framed from the opening pages of the novel. Hurston's text has warned the reader from these same early pages of its potential for destruction, teasing itself with the "ships at a distance" puzzle that sets the narrative tone. This often-quoted paragraph (perhaps so much so because its ambiguity invites a variety of critical comment) is a linguistic trope, a tease. It is language used to tell on, to signify upon, itself. It warns the reader through such signification that here is a text that talks its own structures into existence. I think it is less important to try to discover what Hurston's opening paragraphs mean than it is to point out that these paragraphs signal a text with an internal force that will gather strength through its manipulations of language. Gates's observation of the importance of this text's structure clarifies its importance:

> Hurston . . . has made *Their Eyes Were Watching God* into a paradigmatic signifying text, for this novel resolves that implicit tension between the literal and the figurative contained in standard English usages of the term "signifying." *Their Eyes* represents the black trope of signifying both as thematic matter and as a rhetorical strategy of the novel itself.[9]

I would take Gates's point further and assert that *Eyes* represents a vocal structure that is something more basic than "strategy." He observes that Janie, the protagonist, "gains her voice, as it were, in her husband's store not only by engaging with the assembled men in the ritual of signifying . . . but also by openly signifying upon her husband's impotency." I support this statement with an amendation important to my thesis of voice: Janie gains her voice from the available voice of the text and subsequently learns to share it with the narrator, as I will demonstrate in the chapters that follow. This is a vital extension of Gates's discussion of *Eyes*. I must credit the voice gained to the structure itself. Certainly the traditions of signifying belong to a black community, but Hurston has made them belong to a literary text in ways that empower them to take on their own life forms. This is a tradition of voice let loose in *Jonah* and re-merged to the literary text in *Eyes*. I think it is the same voice because Hurston uses it as character—investing it with active power. Sometimes her "word" is a teasing ambiguity; other times, it is an innocent bystander. But lest we fail to take it seriously, it returns in a whirlwind to exact its due on the very world it had created in the beginning. We know this is so because in the final pages of the novel, which are really the opening pages because this novel is a flashback (another show of power by the recursive word), Janie talks to her friend Phoeby, telling her what she must tell those who criticize what she has done with her life. "Then you must *tell* [emphasis added] them," Janie says, and if we have attended to that power of the word to speak itself into being, we know that Janie too has learned that through telling her spirit will rest fulfilled. "Love is lak de sea," she tells Pheoby, while the narrative voice finishes the image that opened the novel and speaks of Janie pulling "in her horizon like a great fish-net" and calling her soul "to come and see." The images of water and air collapse in these final pages; the wind turns peaceable and waits for its next embodiment.

Having exacted their earthly due in Hurston's first two novels, her words go on to establish a direct link with god and his magicians, like Moses and angels on the Suwannee. The word as allegory is the basis of *Moses, Man of the Mountain*, and were I to use a more ancient and intimate term, then I would "tell" that the allegory is Hoodoo. Most important, *Moses* begins as an oral text, but since the word has developed just about all the strength it can through oracy, it does not end this way. In this book, characters talk about language, speculating, for example, that Moses is trying to use some "psychology" by talking the way they talk. Characters use language as a means of gaining power as they learn the spells and incantations that will invest them with the wizardry of Damballah. But Moses learns his strongest words from the *Book of Thoth*, recommended to him by a palace stableman who taught him the language of animals. This is an important juncture for Hurston's oral texts. Here we know she has acknowledged that within the word's creative potential is the birthing of the literary text, for within the mythology of the *Book of Thoth* is the story of the gift of writing to humankind. The oral word has embraced the written at this juncture, and Hurston's textual explorations of the word face *completio.*

Moses learns from this book the enchantments and secrets of the natural world. Although his teacher Jethro taught him how to free the Israelites, Moses' more important lessons come from that ancient book that facilitates his surpassing the knowledge and abilities of his teacher. To assure that the reader does not miss the power invested in Moses, the novel talks (signifies) to itself in a long passage that repeats the "crossing over" phrase enough to make it litany, chant and incantation:

> Moses had crossed over. He was not in Egypt. He had crossed over and now he was not an Egyptian. He had crossed over. The short sword at his thigh had a jewelled hilt but he had crossed over and so it was no longer the sign of birth and power. He had crossed over, so he sat down on a rock. . . . He had crossed over so he was not of the house of Pharoah. He did not own a palace because he had crossed over. He did not have an Ethiopian princess for a wife. He had crossed over. He did not have enemies to strain against his strength and power. He had crossed over. He was subject to no law. . . . He had crossed over. The sun who was his friend and ancestor in Egypt was arrogant and bitter in Asia. He had crossed over. He felt as empty as a post hole for he was none of the things he once had been. He was a man sitting on a rock. He had crossed over.[10]

Viewed from outside the text, this passage contains all the references and relationships to black sociohistorical experience that are apparent in the patterning of the religious call-and-response, the parody on passing/crossing over[11] and the literary implication of his having been granted, like the convert in that gospel song, a "new life." Within the text, this recursion serves a different function. Highlighted through this repetition of words is the flight of the text after itself, a building of cyclic power like a gyre, tightening and winding its coils into a massive energy and circulating this power into the rock Moses sits on that is an image of the mountain he is to claim. It is a structure at the pinnacle of the semiological relationship between the signifier and that which is signified upon, because, in the coiling, the distinction between the two is lost. The text signifies, speaks to itself and the recursive loops focus back onto the linguistic acts that created the actors. Hurston begins that lengthy passage by telling that Moses' place was not in Egypt. She closes it by telling that he had found his place, and symbolically the place for his word—on a rock. The ground of Egypt, his figurative and literal motherland, became the ground of his being through the text's own incantation in a story about the power of magic words, written and spoken.

Hurston's last published novel, *Seraph on the Suwannee*, is a somber story. Its words are encumbered by clashes of class and gender, and its text is weighted by psychological portraiture. This is a novel that exposes. Its word "reveals" and "tells on" a woman's repression and submission and a family's dissolution. Although Arvay's search for love is "knowing and doing," she has no real idea how to go about this. These words signify her need for spiritual rather than physical activation to replace the emotional lethargy that disables her. I think the appropriate focus in this novel is on the words "knowing and doing" because they embody the elements of Hurston's most powerful linguistic structures. In addition to being a novel of self-actualization, a novel about white people and a novel of contradictory impotence, this is also a novel about direction. The words of its text are tightly controlled and they are quite different from the lyrical modes of Hurston's earlier narration. These are words that refuse to share or alternate perspectives between character, narrator and reader. They are not sheltering words because these white people come to represent distance from the soul rather than nearness to it. Evidence of this evolution into a restricting and exacting word is clear if we admit that Hurston lost control of this text. Although she probably wanted to write a story in which Arvay would assume angelic potential, the text eventually directs itself. Despite or in spite of Hurston's philosophical "stance" on the issues of her story, it became relatively unimportant in the face of a subject who was fatefully destined to lose ownership of the word. I think it entirely possible that Hurston did believe that Arvay Henson Meserve was angelic. She tried to portray her this way when she wrote: "Who shall ascend into the hill of the Lord? And who shall stand in

His holy place? Arvay *thought* [emphasis added] that it would be herself,"[12] but it is clear that she never quite reaches this potential and that she remains a servant to the words that craft her. Throughout the text Arvay struggles to *do* and *be* in ways that won't cause her spirit to come back at her, exposing her guilt and causing her pain. But Hurston keeps after Arvay, burdening her with guilt and a deformed child and a husband whose name implies servitude rather than solace. I don't think that Hurston really liked Arvay or that she felt this character could be saved through a discovery of her self. The text reminds us that Arvay "departed from herself" and that time spent with her husband only "appeared" to be like time in Paradise. The seraphim that finally "hovers" over Jim Meserve at the end of the novel is a poor substitute for the potential of that celestial metaphor.

This book, whether it was Hurston's intention or not, works out a theme of inadequacy seeking itself and finding itself, remained earthbound with a distorted vision of Paradise. Contrast, for example, the imagery of *Eyes* where pictures of love and light are vibrant and activated with their acquisition of the human spirit of Janie. In this text, the light and the word are one and they rejoice in her spirit. Thus powerfully invested, Janie "calls" her soul to share her epiphany. But spiritually poor Arvay was still outer-directed and therefore in conflict with a word that pleaded for her internalization. Unlike the assertive Janie, Arvay does what "the big light tells her." Here is no participant-structure. Here is the dominating word, invigorating itself though its directive power and at the same time telling its fate to make modern metaphors that illustrate nothing so much as man's distance from the creative word. Hurston ends this text with the note that Arvay "met the look of the sun with confidence," announcing, in image if not in fact, that she was ready to serve from her distance, but not to own her soul. She is no Janie Starks, and, although Hurston might have intended for her to be, her whiteness, which translates for me as a lack of ownership of language and idea, makes such soulful epiphany impossible. If Hurston was unaware of this as she began the novel, the cautious, controlling word assured that this would be the literary result. The words shift away from the characters of her black universes because her characters are of a world where neither community nor "place" has value. They cannot carry the imagery of her black texts because they are different sorts of vessels. Hurston, in acknowledging the versatility of the word, submits control of her artistry to this restructured text that speaks to itself in a language that manipulates its characters. The rich, complex imagery of the earlier "speaker texts" from which *Seraph* has evolved fits the complexities of those texts' characters. They shuttle between the physical and spiritual worlds in search of themselves. In *Seraph*, Arvay has no worlds to access but her mother's house (that she later burns) and the swampy outreaches of the home her husband prepares for her. What, then, is the appropriate response of text to such sterility? Probably exactly the wasteland we find in *Seraph*. Hurston has not written a white text, nor has she written a black one in "whiteface," a notion Howard supports in her comment that "Hurston never leaves the folk milieu in *Seraph on the Suwannee*. She does change the color of her characters but she does not change her themes or environment in any significant way."[13]

What has Hurston done in this text? I would argue that she has changed both color and imagery in ways that shout to her readers. The environments are no longer insular, nurturing and fertile. They are deathlike images of dead values, lost ambition and thwarted goals. Her themes have always been various, and rather than looking at the black novels for a shared theme that grows out of their blackness, and lament this one novel because it cannot fit the black aesthetics of the earlier texts, I would suggest we look at these novels for structures that assert themselves as Hurston's craft enables the word to carry the image whatever its color or potential.

It is valuable and important to understand that each of Hurston's novels is related to the degree that they evidence textual structures that speak of themselves. Such a perspective both clarifies and signals the potential of the textual word as it is specifically endowed through texts that are linked by their craftiness and separated in their crafting.

NOTES

1. Roland Barthes, *Writing Degree Zero* (1953; reprint, Boston: Beacon Press, 1970), p. 80.

2. Ralph Ellison, "The World and the Jug," in *Shadow and Act* (New York: Vintage Books, 1964), p. 140.

3. Roland Barthes writes of the potential for any graphic representation of signification as a "somewhat clumsy" operation that nonetheless is "necessary" for semiological discourse. He then illustrates the attempts of Saussure, Hjelmslev and Lacan to render graphically the relationship between signifier

and signified. See Barthes, *Elements of Semiology* (1964; reprint, Boston: Beacon Press, 1970), pp. 48–49.

4. Barfield's most persuasive discussion on this issue is in his text *Poetic Diction* (1928; reprint, Middletown, Conn.: Wesleyan University Press, 1973), especially the chapters "Meaning and Myth" and "The Making of Meaning (I) and (II)." Other references to the nature of meaning are found in his text, *Speaker's Meaning* (Middletown, Conn.: Wesleyan University Press, 1967) and his chapter "The Texture of Medieval Thought" in *Saving the Appearances: A Study in Idolatry* (New York: Harcourt, Brace and World, 1957).

5. I am indebted to Henry Louis Gates's wonderful essay "The Blackness of Blackness: A Critique of the Sign and the Signifying Monkey" in *Black Literature and Literary Theory* (New York: Methuen, 1984) for framing my thinking on this issue.

6. Walter C. Daniel, *Images of the Preacher in Afro-American Literature* (Washington, D.C.: University Press of America, 1980). Daniel notes the similarity between James Weldon Johnson's "Listen Lord, A Prayer" and Pearson's prayer in this novel.

7. Zora Neale Hurston, *Jonah's Gourd Vine* (1934; reprint, Philadelphia: J. B. Lippincott, 1971), pp. 50, 51.

8. Ibid., pp. 267, 268

9. Gates, p. 290.

10. Zora Neale Hurston, *Moses, Man of the Mountain* (1939; reprint, Urbana: University of Illinois Press, 1984), pp. 103, 104.

11. Hemenway (*Zora Neale Hurston: A Literary Biography* [Urbana: University of Illinois Press, 1977], pp. 269–270) and Lillie Howard (*Zora Neale Hurston* [Boston: Twayne Publishers, 1980], pp. 121–122) both spend time discussing this passage. Hemenway's interpretive thrust is directed toward the "pun" on crossing over as "passing"—being a man transformed, spiritually and physically. Howard cites Hemenway's long passage and notes its thematic similarity to James Weldon Johnson's *Autobiography of an Ex-Coloured Man*.

12. Zora Neale Hurston, *Seraph on the Suwannee* (New York: Charles Scribner's Sons, 1948), p. 68.

13. Howard, *Zora Neale Hurston*, p. 134.

4

The Word Assumes Its Raiment and Other Appropriate Garb

Nommo, the life force, is . . . a spiritual-physical fluidity giving life to everything, penetrating everything, causing everything. . . . Since man has power over the word, it is he who directs the life force. Through the word he receives it, shares it with other beings, and so fulfills the meaning of life. . . . "The word is for all in this world. It must be exchanged, so that it goes and comes, for it is good to receive the forces of life."

—Janheinz Jahn, *Muntu*[1]

In Hurston, the development of character is critically linked to voice. Voice, as the African word *nommo*, indicates creative potential. Hurston's construction of character blends the magic of this African word with the poetry of nature and bodies forth women and men fully invested with the power that union would imply.

Hurston's interest in folklore not only illustrates her interest in linguistic attitudes and customs, but reflects the kinds of information that developed from her academic association with Franz Boas. It also indicates how she, as a member of the race whose "cultural deprivation" was constantly an issue for Euro-American anthropologists, sought to offer an alternative view of her culture through the medium of a literature that celebrated its linguistic complexities. In *Black Literature and Literary Theory*, Gates writes:

> We, the critics of black literary traditions, owe it to those traditions to bring to bear upon their readings any "tool" which . . . enables us to see more clearly the complexities of figuration peculiar to our literary traditions . . . the ways in which language and literature mediate between "reality" . . . and its reflections are both complex and subtle.[2]

Gates's discussion of the complexities of text extends to the political "act" of writing that is implicit in black authorship. Hurston has especially confronted, through her own experiences, the political ramifications of her literature, and it is important to note that at least one consequence of sociopolitical interpretive frames within the black text is, as Gates notes, that "the structure of the black text has been repressed and treated as if it were transparent."[3] Close attention to the text itself has not been the tradition in black critical analysis, and, in consequence, a huge body of potential critical insight has been left uninvestigated.

Hurston's texts are excellent materials for the kind of careful, structural attention that is due black literature. Her academic interests saw themselves reflected in her literature in a very carefully structured way. Not only did the language of her text reveal these interests, but the character of her words—their constructions, their use, their deep structures—built a level of consciousness within the fiction that accessed the rest of her text through complex networks of plot, setting and character. If, as her biographer noted, her folklore "refuted" the stereotypes of her anthropological training, we must also note that her fiction confronted and took issue with these same stereotypes. Although Hurston acknowledged the same anthropological assumptions that translated into cultural racism for the white academics who differentiated race and culture, in her effort to refute genetic racism she did not interpret this differentiation as cultural deficiency.[4] Here, her cultural background pushed her away from what must have been the persuasive influence of Boas on this issue. As a result she was able to celebrate the excellence and value of the cultural differences she found in black African Americans. Because much of this affirmation can be seen through her structuring of the language within her fiction, we must conclude that Hurston's knowledge of the dialect she used in her novels and her academic background combined to fashion a particular kind of political statement as well as a particular kind of textual structure.

It is critical that I point out that Hurston's choice of style and structure in her novels was not a consciously studied, scientific approach. Her autobiography frequently suggested that Hurston's dual roles as a novelist and as a serious social scientist with linguistic interests often conflicted. Her novels were criticized by some reviewers as containing too much folklore; others complained they did not have enough. It seems her audience was looking either for a good narrative or a good folk story. They definitely were not looking for scientific statement. When she organized the mass of folklore data she had collected on her various expeditions for the *Mules and Men* collection, her publishers forced it into a form representing a collection of folklore humorously narrated. There is little to suggest that it is the result of a scientific expedition that included an analysis of the form, function and intent of the folktale. Hurston conceded to this structuring of the research, even encouraging its presentation in that format, hoping that her understanding of its representation of the linguistically competent culture of black Americans would also be the understanding of her audience. The political posture of such a presentation was that it evidenced the different, rather than deficient, culture of black America.

Her combination then, of science and literature, must not be separated by critics who approach Hurston. She never published commentary that indicated her academic understandings of language and culture without presenting her data and evidence in the guise of a highly amusing story or an absorbing novel. Hurston recognized the linguistic systems that complicated the structures of language within the dialect and used those systems to complicate her structures of storytelling. Unfortunately, the data, submerged as it was in such structures, has been either ignored or treated as something separate from the text. Separated, it loses its vital connection to the body that nurtures it—the word, in fact, loses its genesis.

THE NARRATIVE FUNCTION

The narrator's role is the key to understanding Hurston's system that blended her knowledge of literary universes and linguistic systems. The system grew from the dichotomy she exemplified. As a member of the culture she closely scrutinized, she could abandon her academic garb and become a member of the group of people who sat on the steps of Joe Clarke's store in Eatonville (an image that frequently appears in her fiction) exchanging lies and telling stories with the best of them. The same spirit who, when coached by Boas or Melville Herskovits of Columbia, would prowl the streets of Harlem with calipers in hand, stopping any black person she wished, and ask to measure the size of their skulls, would join the storytelling group in Eatonville, shedding the vestiges of her formal education and status. In *Mules and Men* she wrote:

> From the earliest rocking of my cradle, I had known about the capers Brer Rabbit is apt to cut.... But it was fitting me like a tight chemise. I couldn't see it for wearing it. It was only when I was... away from my native surroundings, that I could... stand off and look at my garment. Then I had to have the spy-glass of Anthropology to look through.[5]

She performs a similar operation, which Hemenway refers to as a "dissociation of sensibility," with the narrator's role in her fiction. On many occasions the narrator is objectively scrutinizing the characters, revealing more to the reader than the characters know about themselves. But, as the prose progresses, she allows the narrator to become almost the subject of the text. The narrative voice blends into the character's linguistic style so closely (or the character's style becomes its), that it frequently is difficult to separate the two.

Wayne Booth's *Rhetoric of Fiction* includes a discussion that describes the possibilities for the narrative voice in fiction.[6] I have structured Booth's analysis to illustrate how Hurston's use of narrative falls outside of these traditionally defined roles and why an alternative structure must be proposed for her novels. Booth describes, in terms that include "Dramatized and Undramatized, Privilege and Reliability," how each type of narration functions for the text. Hurston's narrative voice is one that functions within the story, a category that Booth assigns two possibilities. The "inside" narrative voice is either "dramatized" or "undramatized." But neither of Booth's descriptions for these voices fits the narrator Hurston has developed. Within Booth's description of the "Restricted Narrative View" there are categories that include Hurston's narrators. Figure 1 illustrates the function of Hurston's narrative voices alongside the more traditional structures described by Booth.[7]

The disembodied nature of the narrative voice gives it a kind of Faulknerian purpose: it presides over the activity of the novel, it is

FIGURE 1
Inside Narrative Structures in "Dramatized" and "Restricted" Modes as Compared to Inside Narrative Structures in Hurston's Texts

	DRAMATIZED	RESTRICTED	HURSTON
IDENTITY IN THE STORY	a character	not a character	not a character
VOICE	first person	third person	third person
ACCESS TO CHARACTER'S CONSCIOUSNESS	access only to self	access to consciousness of one character or a community of characters through whose perceptions he conveys the story	same, but offers perspectives of the characters that they are to realize later
PRESENCE	dominates story	submerges his vision into the characters whose perspectives serve as the narrative focus	works toward a blend of consciousness with character, urging, like a character itself, the development of such awareness
RELIABILITY	frequently unreliable because its self-knowledge is imperfect	ranges from reliable to unreliable, depending on its association with characters whose consciousness it reveals and on the presence or absence of clues that negate or affirm implicit attitudes or values	fully reliable because its purpose is to lead the character to share the knowledge it has of him

omniscient, and it functions as a link between the conscious and visible activity of the novel and unconscious, passive awareness. This division between narrator and character can be best explained using linguistic terminology. The narrator, as the deep structure of the novel, represents the underlying competence of a character who is eventually brought to a realization of self. The character, as the surface structure, only externally participates in the text until this level of self-knowledge is attained. Hurston does not allow a character's underlying competence to be exhibited until, through a series of activities that structure the literary areas of plot and theme, he comes to a degree of self-knowledge that matches the narrative understanding of him.[8] These activities involve a soul-searching on the part of the character and are accompanied by his linguistic silence. The narrative voice is dominant during these silences.

Because all of Hurston's novels are stories of journeys toward self-awareness and actualization, the external voices of character gradually blend into the narrative structures in each of them, relinquishing themselves to its greater knowledge and finally blending into its deep-structure competence. The transition is gradual, and the final marriage of voices is accomplished almost without the reader's awareness.

Why does this happen? It could be that Hurston was unconsciously assigning to the narrator the tradition that the folktale generated. The "essence of the folk tale is its easy narrative element, its story-telling, yarn-spinning quality which makes of disbelief belief and wonder."[9]

The folk story is initiated first by one of the storytellers in a group assembled on a porch, in a work place or a "jook-joint." "Lemme tell you why... or how..." Or, "Y'all want to know how come... so Ah'm gointer tell you." This storyteller then makes a subtle shift to narrator-participant, a voice that no longer acknowledges the group of listeners but fully participates in the unfolding of the story's events. Dialogue and narration have equal value in the story. In this structure, the storyteller is both the generator of the story and the cultural benefactor of the mythology the story details. The story's surface structure supports these voices: storyteller, narrator, and characters'. The story's deep structure assumes one blended voice: the black mythology that owns the words.

It seems that Hurston's novels, in an acknowledgment of their folk roots, also recognize this deep-structure voice. In the novels, the voice will eventually release its knowledge to the character and blend its consciousness with the protagonist. For someone who was trained in anthropology and who did her field work recording folk literature, it should not seem unusual that the structures in her longer fiction are similar to the elements of story within the folk tradition.

The Narrative Role in Novelistic Structures

The dialogue in the first sections of Hurston's novels establishes the history and tone of the characters who are presented. In these sections, the characters introduce themselves, interact and set a stage for the events that will occur. Sometimes it is the task of the narrator to set this stage. But the narrative voice in these opening sections does more than simply comment and connect. It seems to take, for this brief moment, a role similar to one Booth assigns the "Outside Narrators," except that this voice is almost like a person, a character standing back and making observations like the one opening *Their Eyes Were Watching God*: "Ships at a distance have every man's wish on board. For some they come in with the tide. For others they sail forever on the horizon, never out of sight, never landing until the Watcher turns his eyes away in resignation, his dreams mocked to death by Time. That is the life of men."[10] For four more paragraphs, this voice philosophizes like a distant and wise observer, and then its vision disappears. Its reemergence is not without this same philosophical perspective that allowed it to say of the people who sit on the porches in late evening that they "made burning statements with questions, and killing tools out of laughs. It was mass cruelty. A mood come alive. Words walking without master; walking altogether like harmony in a song." Except for the fact that Hurston's words do have her as their master, the character of the collected words of her novels is very much like her description above. They are characters because they are words "come alive." The narrative voice that works like this one establishes a relationship within the characters rather than outside of them.

Most frequently, the narrative relationship established with the character who is to come to self-actualization within the course of the story complements this character with parallels drawn between him and nature. It is a choice that grounds the text in African mythology and does so to enable the dialogue of the characters to be surrounded with some measure of the truth that they will eventually come to recognize.

Whatever deceit, trickery or ignorance obfuscates the soul, nature remains an image that is constant, truthful and right.

In a discussion of Toni Morrison's novels, Barbara Christian identifies a principle that Hurston illustrates as she structures her narrative voices. Christian writes of the link between the community and nature, a link that is viable in Hurston as well. She writes of "Nature" as a "physical or spiritual force, one that can or cannot be affected by human forces."[11] For Morrison, as well as for Hurston, it is critical for characters to acknowledge the potential of nature, to recognize its role in their communities and to accord it due respect. Not to do so would mean that survival is threatened. Following this perspective we should recognize early that Jody Starks's tearing down the natural environment to erect his town in *Their Eyes Were Watching God* is tantamount to suicide. Hurston was not unaware of this link. The man Janie loved, Tea Cake, followed the land and its cycles as a migrant worker, letting nature and its seasons direct him. Through their imagery, the words in Hurston's novels represent respect for such African valuing of the natural/spiritual world.

When Hemenway identifies a "contradiction" at the center of *Jonah's Gourd Vine*, that "John creates poetry . . . but cannot find the words to secure his own personal grace"[12] he underscores the lack of unity between the voice of the spiritual/natural world and the character who has not yet found "grace." Hurston's system, however, moves her characters toward this unity and identifies this need for movement by a narrative voice that does own such awareness. Following this perspective, John's sermons can be seen as a narrator speaking through him, the one who possesses the knowledge toward which the action of the novel compels this character. John himself asserts that "When Ah speak tuh yuh from dis pulpit, dat ain't me talkin', dat's de voice uh God spekin' thru me. When the voice is thew, ah jus' uhnother one uh God's crumblin' clods."[13]

After the separation between the narrator's vision and the character's point-of-view has been established, the narrative voice works to establish a blend between its activity and the activity of the characters it has introduced. It is no longer as apparent, at this stage, where the narrative voice begins and the characters take over. Commentary is blended neatly together with comment. Hurston's first novel, *Jonah*, seems to bend over backward to establish this point—that language is a controlling element in one's life. If we do not anticipate that character is revealed in Hurston not only through the story structure, but through the linguistic structure as well, then her novels may seem confusing in the way that *Jonah* does for Hemenway, who noted that the separation of "confused self from inspired utterance" not only frustrated the character John, but the text as well.[14] Viewing the structure of voice as a progression of stages that Hurston uses to develop the text makes such separation inspired instead of confusing.

The blend that the narrative voice eventually seeks between the character's utterance and its own is documented in the sermons of *Jonah*. It is because God speaks through John on these occasions that we cannot expect him to have the power to recognize the ambivalence between his external actions and his internal motivations—symbolized in the deep structures of his language. With this purpose in mind, to illustrate that John has not yet come to the position of self-awareness, the narrative commentary remains distinct from John's external activities and only blends the images of nature and the settings that already hold some degrees of truth. The sermons where God (narrative truth) speaks through John are Hurston's hints to the reader of the existence of this structure. The narrative that relates the reaction of John Pearson's congregation, after hearing a sermon he constructed to extricate himself from the accusations of adultery, artistically blends the soul-felt forgiveness of the congregation with the symbolic nature of his position: "The church surged up, a weeping wave about him. . . . His weight seemed nothing in many hands while he was roughly, lovingly forced back into his throne-like seat. After a few minutes of concerted weeping he moved down to the communion table and in a feeling whisper went thru the sacrifice of a God."[15] The narration works to blend voices in this way also in *Eyes*:

> She was stretched on her back beneath the pear tree soaking in the alto chant of the visiting bees, the gold of the sun and the panting breath of the breeze when the inaudible voice of it all came to her. She saw a dust-bearing bee sink into the sanctum of a bloom; the thousand sister calyxes arch to meet the love embrace from root to tiniest branch creaming in every blossom and frothing with delight. . . . Then Janie felt a pain remorseless sweet that left her limp and languid.[16]

The dialogue that dominates the second half of this novel is fused with the voice of the narrator and is different in this respect from the dialogue of the early novel in which narrative and character's voices were clearly distinct. This has prompted comments like Hemenway's, who suggests that the persona of the narrator changes inexplicably toward the end of the novel. But the theme of this novel, the growth into self-awareness, could not have been better illustrated than by Janie's growth toward the awareness the narrator has held throughout the text. Her "poetic self-realization"[17] is indicated through a growth toward narrative knowledge that has her own voice growing closer and closer to the poetry of the narrative voice as she moves toward her own self-awareness. Narrative voice works for this blend with character so that the final achievement is not sudden, but a smooth development of the internal perspectives of character. At one stage of the novel, it is difficult to tell whether the narrative voice is character or comment: "But here come Bootsie, Teodie and Big 'oman down the street making out they are pretty by the way they walk. They have got that fresh new taste about them like young mustard greens in the spring."[18] When describing the activity on the porch of Jody Starks's store, the narrator seems to instigate the action "and the young men on the porch are just bound to tell them about it and buy them some treats."[19] This passage is more like dialogue than narration—an example of the blending narrative voice. When the narrative activity and the activity of the characters are so closely merged, this type of paragraph is the artistic result.

In *Moses*, this voice is an even deeper blend of the character and narrator. Hurston uses little actual dialogue here. The structure of the midsections is primarily internal and allows the narrator to write the thoughts of the character as if they were active voice and a substitution for dialogue. Again, Hurston uses narrative structures that read as if they were dialogue, and, only after some attention to the text, does the absence of the structural marks of dialogue assure the reader that no character is speaking. Hurston uses an abundance of poetic devices on these occasions, an appropriate accompaniment for the commentary the narrator offers: "The years went by with a loping gait. A profound calm took up in the face of Moses. It grew rugged like the mountain but held its power inside. . . . He lived on the mountain, in the desert, beside streams, feeding his mind on Nature."[20] In this section of her text, there is only a thin line between the description and analysis. Hurston has indicated that the blending voice of narration is propelling the character closer to its own knowledge. Finally, the narrative voice succeeds in bringing the character or the external action of the novel to its internal realization of truth. This stage of Hurston's fiction involves a complete departure from artistic blend and a takeover of the tone and attitude of the narrative. Here, the concept of tone is critical. Earlier narrative voices establish for the reader the narrative point-of-view. It is not an awareness the protagonist carries because it has had deeper and naturally supported insight into character from the earliest pages of the novel. Neither can character comment on circumstances in the narrative manner. The intrusion of the narrative in the earliest pages of Hurston's fiction is clear and undisguised. It is easy, at this stage, to isolate the explicative tone and intention of the voice.

In *Jonah*, for example, the narrative intervention reveals relationships that become important to the plot in sections like: "The children came leaping in, in tense, laughing competition." In another section of this early narrative, the voice uses events inside and outside of the home to render symbolically the feelings of animosity and conflict within the family: "In the frenzied silence, Amy noticed that the rain had ceased; that the iron kettle was boiling; that a coon dog struck a trail way down near the Creek, and was coming nearer, singing his threat and challenge."[21]

The sarcastic and ironic tone of the narrator in the opening pages of *Seraph* admonishes the reader not to take Avray Henson seriously as it unsympathetically and nearly derisively describes her peculiarities and quirks: "Arvay's tearful speech followed the usual pattern, and everybody said it was just fine.... Five years had passed since Arvay had turned her back on the world.... It was not too difficult for her, because the community soon put Arvay Henson down as queer, if not a little 'tetched.' "[22]

By the time Hurston's novels reach the blending voice of narration, it is possible to separate the distinct points-of-view—the various characters' and the narrative. Analysis of the final narrative voice reveals that the characters have submitted themselves to the more powerful knowledge of the narrator.

In *Jonah*, John Pearson finally grows wise to Hattie's Hoodoo and bemoans the loss of his first wife Lucy with the same wisdom the narrator blended into the earlier sections of the novel:

Look lak ah been sleep. Ah ain't never meant tuh marry you... but here us is married, Hattie, how come that? Suddenly a seven-year-old picture came before him. Lucy's bright eyes in the sunken face. Helpless and defensive. The look. Above all, the look! John stared at it in fascinated horror for a moment. The sea of the soul, heaving after a calm, giving up its dead.[23]

It is the final stage of his awareness. The symbolic suggestion that he had been "asleep" during the events of the novel, the events that were mainly concerned with the activities of his body, suggest that he was for this time without his soul. Only after he drags the depths of the sea does he retrieve his soul. The linguistic correlation that is possible here suggests that language as a behavioral manifestation is not enough to account for motivation. We need the deeper structure of language, its soul, to understand our performances.

Moses acquires the knowledge of the voice and yearns for it to tell him more. "He wanted to ask God and Nature questions.... The Voice should welcome him and speak of... things like the mysteries of sea and sky and air."[24]

In different fashions, each of Hurston's novels involves a search for truth that can terminate in some recognition of internal sin or weakness or in fulfillment after this weakness has been rectified. Janie finds the fulfillment of love, actually self-love, that she sought throughout the novel. During her search, the narrative sections voice her unhappiness for her, at one point as a "feeling of coldness and fear" that make her feel "far away from things and lonely." Janie has not had the strength of character or the knowledge of soul to voice these fears and actualize them so that she could then confront them. Her actions, as well as her dialogue, have been superficial. But the revelations and criticisms of the narrator fill in the deep structure for her and eventually give voice to her spirit. The closer she comes to recognizing and acknowledging her feelings, the more the spirit struggles to the surface. The conveyer of these emotions is the narrative voice, pushing itself to control the activity and the thought in the novel. Shortly before the death of Jody, Janie begins to recognize the existence of this spiritual force. The narrative voice tells us that "the years took all the fight out of Janie's face," but that after her husband's death she stops "reaching outside" herself for survival and that the "things of death" could not "reach inside to disturb her calm." She finds internal peace.

The final narrative voice in this novel is difficult to distinguish from Janie's own. The blend of this section is the result of her internalizing her passions and desires and finding that she can control her own destiny. The dialect and marks of dialogue distinguish Janie's speech from the standard prose of the narrator. Other than this distinction, they speak for each other. Her language becomes poetic, as the narrative language has been throughout the novel. Following the tragedy of her lover's death, she explains her love to her friend Phoeby:

> Dey gointuh make "miration" cause mah love didn't work lak they love, if dey ever had any. Then you must tell 'em dat love ain' somethin lak uh grindstone dat's de same thing everywhere and do de same thing tuh everything it touch. Love is lak de sea. Its uh movin' thing, but still and all, it takes its shape from de shore and it's different with every shore.[25]

It is significant that Hurston does not give this passage to the narrator, thereby asserting that the dialect, contrary to what her contemporaries in the fields of anthropology and linguistics were saying, could hold and communicate such abstractions, and, further, that this thought comes from the deepest levels of our complex consciousnesses. It appears when we allow our souls to speak for us.

This wise Janie is a far cry from the obedient granddaughter and wife of the early pages of the novel and the subservient wife of Mayor Starks in the midsection. The bond that narrator and protagonist now share has dissolved the boundary between surface structures and deep structures. Language and character are fully synthesized.

This goal of synthesis is as apparent in *Jonah*. The immediate and first effects of narrative blend cause Rev. Pearson to temporarily lose his voice. It is as if internalization takes place, as it did with Janie, with a putting aside of outward things: "John said nothing. His words had been very few since his divorce. He was going about learning old truths for himself as all men must. . . . The world had suddenly turned cold. . . . Oh for the wings, for the wings of a dove! That he might see no more what men's faces held."[26] When John is able to loose himself of the fearful burden of Hattie, recognizing at last the "mojo" she had worked to keep him under her power, he achieves the first stage of freedom. It remains for him to recognize his soul. John's recurrent dreams (the subconsciousness asserting itself) of his first wife Lucy are significant. Lucy is the only one, other than the narrative voice, who understands John's motivation. She knows that his fleshly cravings in no way obviate his belief in God. She is able to know this because her outlook is more cognizant of the original spirit that is whole in nature and reflected in man. She has looked upon her husband with scorn because of his hypocrisy and its painful effect on their relationship. She knows he will not understand that it is possible to reconcile the conflicts of spirit, flesh and religion. John, on the other hand, never sees the imbalance, the unnatural; he champions the separation of the man in the pulpit and the man on the porch. Hurston notes that the preacher maintains this dichotomy in her letter to James Weldon Johnson. She wrote that the preacher was a poet but also: "a human, and, as such, beset with the burdens and temptations of human existence. As poet his power rests in his projection of the Word. As bearer of the Word, he is both the Son of God and the Son of Man. His tragic dilemma is that he can be fully neither one nor the other; especially on the basis of some abstract morality."[27]

Hurston recognizes the hypocrisy of the morality, but does not allow John this same recognition, perhaps because she is herself unsure of its workability in his community. Her assertion that Christian "morality" demands artificial separation of body and spirit does not translate into a sharing of this awareness with her protagonist. Language in this text holds the truths for John, but the spiritual and ancient voices, like the narrative voice in this novel, forever function within the linguistic/mythic deep structure, never gaining consciousness.

At this point the reader, the narrator and John all know he is fighting an unresolvable battle. His final church, Pilgrim Rest, symbolizes the end of this spiritual journey. He battles the flesh once more (in the form of the seductive Ora), loses again, and on his way home from church is struck by a train and instantly killed. Death resolves for him the conflict he was unable to mediate. The narrator of *Jonah* tells us that his funeral drum, reminiscent of that African spirit that John denied through Christianity, was the voice of Death that promises nothing, speaks only with tears and of the past. "He wuz uh man, and nobody knowed 'im but God" is the final pronouncement of this novel. His "access," as Hemenway defines it, to a "pre-Christian memory" evoked through the language of the narrator is his only real potential for salvation.[28]

In the final pages of *Moses*, Moses, like Janie and unlike John Pearson, does achieve the poetic understanding of the omniscient narrator. For the first time his ascent of the mountain, his final journey, is not at the request of another. First it was Jethro who taught him that there was magic to be learned from the mountain and begged him to go up.

Then God beckoned him there to receive his wisdom and instructions. But this final ascent was on his own initiative. Once there he realized, as the narrative voice had known and illustrated all along, that "no man may make another free. Freedom was something within. The outside signs were just the signs and symbols of the man inside."[29] Again, we find the narrative voice bringing us this internal realization. It is important to the premise of this blending narrative voice that Moses, in his final mountaintop ruminations, realizes that in the people of Israel whom he has brought to the foot of the mountain, God "had a voice." This gift of language, the voice to express God and spirit, becomes Moses' ultimate gift to the people. As if to underscore the acquisition of power Moses has finally and fully assumed, the narrative voice explains that the "dimming sunlight gave him inside vision." Connected in this natural way to his soul, Moses is ready to "ask God and Nature" questions instead of receiving and conveying their instructions.

Arvay, in the last pages of *Seraph*, realizes what her husband had been trying to accomplish with their marriage. He had not wanted to settle for only the outward shows of affection, care and concern without an inner devotion and commitment. Arvay could never manage to extend her soul to the man she married because she has not been in touch with it herself. Her doubts, fears and mistrust have had too firm a hold on her spirit for love and trust or even independent self-assertiveness to intrude. There is a fierce struggle between the narrative voice and Arvay throughout the novel. The voice indicates the love and intense devotion Jim held for Arvay; even though the words of the name "me-serve" she eventually shared with him imply that self-possessiveness like his was a more appropriate goal for this woman. In this story, the swamp, which becomes the burial ground for her idiot son, is the symbol of the muddied and confused field of Arvay's feelings. Sexual repression, represented through the phallic imagery of a snake that threatens her husband, is another representation of her denial of her natural self. That the images of nature in this novel are negative and threatening is further evidence of the ravages of nature when we refuse to acknowledge her spirit in us. These incidents, symbols and images are resolved in the blend of the final pages. Once more we find narrator and protagonist speaking for each other. Arvay realizes that: "All that had happened to her, good or bad, was a part of her own self and had come out of her. Within her own flesh were many mysteries.... What was in you was bound to come out and stand."[30] As the narrative voice described her feeling it also spoke of her actions. There was no longer a struggle between the two; Arvay concedes to the power of the voice, again an image of the sun, and although she does not share the voice's wisdom, she no longer engages it in battle.

The symbols employed by the narrative voice in Hurston seem to be a conscious attempt on her part to pull us beneath the surface of the dialogue and indicate to the reader where the characters have to go to resolve the conflicts and finish the journeys each has begun. When she labels John Pearson a poet who "manipulates words in order to convey to others the mysteries," we should understand that the emphasis on poetic devices in narrative voices serves the same purpose, and that, as author, Hurston acknowledged her task to structure a system that united character with the creative potential of their words. Both her readers and the characters must reach toward this understanding.

The characters of Hurston's novels seem to be developed along very specific patterns. Through thoughtful blending of several elements, the total character is realized. In her stories, four elements are significant in the blend that defines character. They are: Narrative Voice, Setting, Interpersonal Relationships and Language.

Narrative Voice. Because the narrative voice often serves as spokesperson for a character who has not yet found his own voice, this voice is often our first clue to character. Although the blend of elements is essential to the full character, the early voice of the narrator can reveal some important aspects of its development. In *Moses*, the narrator tells us early, when Moses is still a young prince in training, that: "He was a born trooper.... There was something about him that assured them he was a companion to be relied on in times of danger. They wanted to follow him into whatever escapade he thought up. He was the young men's choice for a leader."[31] This voice gives us reason to understand why, at a much later point of the novel, this man could convince an entire nation to follow him for years into the desert that lay beyond the Red Sea.

The history in these beginning pages prepares the reader for the important element of Setting in this text. Because the conflict between Pharoah and Moses and the Egyptian and Hebrew peoples is so central to this novel, it is important for these opening pages to establish a tone that prepares the reader for the underlying conflicts explored in the novel. Such lines as the following illustrate this point:

> They had trampled on the proud breast of Egyptian liberty for more than three hundred years. But the gods had used the courage of the real Egyptians to conquer and expel those sheep-herding interlopers. . . . All he [Pharoah] had required of them was that they work and build him a few cities here and there to pay back some of the wealth they had so ruthlessly raped from the helpless body of Egypt when she was in no position to defend herself.[32]

The early narrative voice usually acts to describe the freedom that must be achieved by or for the protagonist in the novel. Janie, in *Eyes*, struggles to free herself from the control of Jody Starks. Moses is learning the wizardry of Damballah to help wrench the Hebrews' freedom from the hands of Pharoah. Arvay, in *Seraph*, is fighting the emotional reins of her idiot son as well as her many levels of guilt. In *Jonah*, John Pearson is embroiled in the hypocrisy of church and flesh. The task of the narrative voice in these sections is to internalize the characters' awareness successfully so they may realize their own potential and value. In the midsections of text the complications of plot emerge and illustrate the conflicts the characters must overcome before they can be self-reliant. Here the narrative voice often provides structural clues that indicate how close the characters are to reaching their individual awareness of self.

Setting. Setting provides perhaps the most poetic element of character development. This element must achieve the distinction of putting character into a situation that serves as his leitmotiv, functioning like the thematic interplay of a sonata. Through the various shifts of this theme from major to minor key, from andante to allegro tempos, the theme continues to be recognized. When, in recapitulation, it appears again in its original form, it is a broader, better-defined and fuller statement because of its development. The same can be said of the development of character in Hurston. The setting that is attached to character grows fuller with each change. The final picture of character emerges with the well-established element of setting bound into our vision of this character. For example, when Moses leaves the increasingly hostile company of the Egyptians and crosses the Red Sea for the first time, Hurston describes him as an alienated soul, no longer an Egyptian, bereft of all but the outward signs of birth and power.

He is denied his house, he faces neither friend nor enemy and he is "as an empty post hole, for he was none of the things he once had been." But he was a "man sitting on a rock. He had crossed over." This rock becomes the early symbol of the mountain on which Moses was to regain all and more than he had lost in leaving the Egyptians. The power that he gleaned from this mountain became the strength of the Hebrew children. This symbolic clue, at this early point of the novel, is crucial. It is a symbol carefully developed from the introductory image. As he travels away from the Red Sea and his "rock," he catches his first sight of his mountain.

> He saw it at a distance, lifting its *rocky* [emphasis added] crown above the world, and he was dumbstruck with awe. To him it had its being in grandeur, so it was right and proper to draw itself apart from the surrounding country and hide its mysteries in its heart. It was near; it was far. It called, it forbade. He must believe in gods again, for here was the tomb of a god a thousand times greater than pyramids. No, it was not a vain thing like a pyramid.... It had an aura of clouds upon its brow. This sublime earth form was surely the living-place of a god. It had peace and fury in its face.[33]

This is the setting that serves as backdrop for the most important activity of the novel. Moses and the mountain, as the title of the novel indicates, soon become synonymous.

There is natural setting as dramatic in *Their Eyes Were Watching God*. It is an element attached from the earliest scenes to Janie, who blossoms like the pear tree, and develops maturity and independence, and, indeed, fury, like nature. They separate, each asserting their own power, and join in the final pages as images of light and sun that whisper through her memory, her soul. As Janie becomes more of her "natural" self, that is, less a victim of the whims of others, the setting of the novel moves closer to the natural world. Its movement coincides with Janie's and growth begins at the long-cultivated farm of Logan Killicks. The establishment of those surroundings was about as deliberate as Janie's and Logan's relationship. There is no spontaneity, no gaiety, there are no surprises. From this first marriage, she moves with Jody Starks to Eatonville, a town just being developed from a clearing in Florida. As the plan of the town grows more and more detailed, the relationship between Jody and Janie grows more and more artificial and strained. Jody, promptly upon arrival in Eatonville, begins to build up the town by cutting down the natural environment and taming the wilderness. Simultaneously he sets out to curb what he sees as the "wildness" in Janie's spirit. Eventually he becomes the mayor of the carefully laid-out town and Janie is his silent, carefully controlled and resentful wife, her natural strength and spirit symbolically rendered impotent by the image of her hair hidden behind a cloth handkerchief. Both her self and her spirit are relegated to the back of the store that Jody runs. When Janie escapes this setting and takes off with Tea Cake, we find a very different kind of relationship. He is a free spirit, a sojourning man, traveling wherever work takes him. They follow a migrant trail, moving with the crops and avoiding exerting any control over the natural scheme of their environments. The ironic and bitter climax of this story is that untamed nature, a hurricane, initiates a chain of events that eventually forces Janie to take the life of the only man she has ever loved with her body and her soul. We get some indications of the impending tragedy during the bitter sweep of the storm: "The wind came back with a triple fury and put out the light for the last time. They sat in the company with the others, their eyes straining against the crude walls and their souls asking if He meant to measure their puny might against His. They seemed to be staring at the dark, but their eyes were watching God."[34] Nature has bowed to human forces throughout the novel. Here she shows that she is a power that can control, as well as be controlled. Perhaps her fury is a lesson for Janie, who has been linked with natural imagery throughout the story and who needs to learn the potential strength of her own independence.

Interpersonal Relationships. It is common for a novelist to expand her reader's knowledge of characters through the development of relationships with other characters in the novel. Hurston's works follow this familiar course. However, what is unique in Hurston is that all relationships have a single purpose. They work to establish a dependency that will be eliminated at the point of self-actualization. Her four novels each develop this paradoxically dependent/independent relationship between main and subsidiary characters. Their dependence is usually quite literal. Arvay needs Jim Meserve to care for her, love her and provide for her family. Moses needs Jethro, who functions as the human extension of the mountain, to guide him to the magic wellsprings of the mountain's powers. Janie needs her grandmother, Jody, Logan and Tea Cake to give her the spiritual fuel she needs to examine the quality of her own desires. John Pearson needs Lucy and Hattie to satisfy his physical needs and Lucy to vocalize his spiritual goals. The dependencies of these main characters are all quite real and binding. But their independence in these interpersonal relationships comes about because of their various dependencies. Herein lies the paradox. Arvay's needing Jim leads her to realize that she is a woman who should be serving self. Moses learns through Jethro that the secrets to all magic lie within the mountain. Once he masters these powers, his strength is greater than Jethro's, who has been his mentor. Through his learning, he becomes teacher. Pitiful John Pearson, haunted by Lucy's truths and Hattie's "mojos," takes a flight of independence away from them both. But his flight is into the hands of another protector, Sally. Finally, the ultimate act of liberation is accomplished for him—his death. The reader understands at this point that John will never come to the point of awareness on his own; death is his soul's only salvation.

Language. Hurston uses black dialect, standard usage and literary language to fill out her characters. Each usage, whether standard, dialect or literary, illuminates an event she wishes to underscore in a special manner.

Much of her dialogue between characters is within the grammar defined as a black dialect. Excluded from this is the dialogue between the Hensons and the Meserves, the white characters of *Seraph*. Hurston's usage of dialect is both historical and illustrative. She obviously wished to improve the historical accuracy of her novels by capturing the way folk talked. But what is more important is that through the use of dialect, Hurston revealed the many nuances of meaning and intention carried within its morphophonemic frame.

For example, the newly liberated Hebrews begin grumbling among themselves about the authority Moses seems to have. Moses, who within contemporary definitions is bidialectal, chooses to speak the dialect of the Hebrews to try to settle their differences. He says: "It's no use for me to try to talk any higher court language with these people, I might as well get right down with them."[35] The Hebrews are not unaware of the psychological advantage Moses tries to claim by "talking our language just like we talk it ourselves." They also realize that what makes Moses' attempts humorous and ineffective is "he forgets... and goes back to talking his proper talk when he gets excited." Later, we see evidence in another novel of a character using proportionately more dialect when she gets excited. In addition to a linguistic observation concerning linguistic interference,[36] Hurston is making an observation about character that the reader should not ignore.

Hurston illustrates the instrumentality of language in this type of interchange, especially with someone who is bidialectal. That she is aware of the social benefits and hazards of bidialectalism is revealed in her discussion of the origin of the hostility between the Hebrews and Moses. On a larger scale she has commented that those who attempt to use language they only know superficially will be betrayed by their lack of a deep-structure competence that will assure that they can generate language identical to the native speakers. Sincerity is an emotion that can be measured within linguistic frames.

The use of dialect also functions to deepen the level of communication between characters who share the dialect. This is illustrated in *Eyes*, for example, by the fact that the fewer and fewer standard features the dialect uses means characters are involved more deeply in nuance and exchanges. Conversations on the store's porch between shoppers and proprietors are usually lively and heated exchanges on a variety of topics and people. They are also very deeply marked by the phonemic/etic features of the dialect, indicating that the level of involvement of the participants is full and uninhibited by what was considered "proper" English. The implication is that "proper" English, for speakers whose native language is the black dialect, is an escape from the depths of existence and feelings. It is the difference between language that observes and language that participates. This reasoning may also be associated with the standard English observations of the narrative voice and the dialectal involvement of the characters with their lives. When Janie finally loses all patience with her status as Jody's silent partner, her retribution minces no words: "You big-bellies around here and put out a lot of brag, but 'tain't nothin to it but you' big voice. . . . Talkin' bout me lookin' old! When you pull down yo britches, you look lak de change uh life!"[37] The more hotly involved she is with her diatribe, the less her language resembles the standard one. The more emotional the exchange, the deeper the level of feeling that is expressed, and more dialectal markedness is the result. This holds true in most of the dialect usage for Hurston, and it becomes an important technique in the structuring of the dialogue as an aspect of characterization.

Poetic prose belongs to both the narrator's usually standard usage and the character's dialect. It is important to note that Hurston recognizes the power of dialect to carry eloquently the poetic statement. The preacher as poet illustrates the strength of poetry in dialect in *Jonah*. Unfortunately, much of the strength of the sermon on pages 271 to 281 of the text lies in being able to hear the delivery. The important rhythm and intonational inflections of the sermon are only apparent to those who are familiar both with the dialect and the structure and technique of the black sermon form. But appreciation for the skilled use of metaphor and imagery are accessible to Hurston's general readership. In the following passage from one of Rev. Pearson's sermons, the personified Sun begs God to create man in its image:

> De Sun, Ah!
> Gethered up de fiery skirts of her garments
> And wheeled around de throne, Ah!
> Saying, Ah, make man after me, ha!
> God gazed upon the sun
> And sent her back to her blood-red socket

The moon is surrounded by the silvery images of the sea:

> De moon, ha!
> Grabbed up de reins of de tides
> And dragged a thousand seas behind her...

as Jesus commands his armies:

> And he arose
> And de storm was in its pitch
> And de lightnin' played on His raiments as He stood on the prow of the boat
> And placed his foot upon the neck of the storm
> And spoke to the Howlin' winds
> And de sea fell at His feet like a marble floor
> And de thunders went back in their vault
> Then He set down on de rim of de ship
> And took de hooks of His power
> And lifted de billows in His lap
> And rocked de winds to sleep on His arm
> And said, "Peace, be still."[38]

The sermon on these pages includes the important locutionary marks of its delivery as further indications of its style and force. It is an authentic sermon from one of God's "trombones."[39] Both Hurston and James Weldon Johnson assigned the black preacher the role of poet for the race. "The cosmography of Afro-American religion," writes Walter C. Daniel, "appears from the very first line of *Jonah.* 'God was grumbling His thunder and playing the zig-zag lightning thru his fingers.' " Daniel calls it the "religion of his ethnicity" and notes that this cultural cloak conflicts with the Christian cloak he represented himself as wearing.[40] The ethnicity that Daniel identifies is sustained throughout the text by the dialect. Even though the message and conflict of the novel support the Christian cloak, the language of the character, whether he sermonizes or sins, reflects the ethnicity that unifies his spirit to the non-Western world.

The poetry of the dialect is not only exhibited in sermons, but in dialogue as well. Just after Janie has described her love as being like the sea, "uh moving thing . . . tak[ing] its shape from de shore it meets," the narrative voice matches Janie's poetic prose: "Janie mounted the stairs with her lamp. The light in her hand was like a spark of sun stuff. . . . The kiss of his [Tea Cake's] memory made pictures of love and light again against the wall. Here was peace. She pulled in her horizon like a great fish net."[41]

For John Pearson, the force of the narration begs for him to realize that he has sacrificed his manhood for his Christianized spirit. For Arvay Meserve, the interpersonal relationships of her familial and marital ties help demonstrate her need for self-actualization. Janie is victim in every relationship but the final one. There, the overwhelming forces of nature assert their control, but they do not rob her of her inner peace. Moses, too, finds strength and receives his knowledge and power from God-in-Nature: "The moon in its reddest mood became to him a standing place for his feet and the sky ran down so close to gaze on Moses that the seven great suns of the Universe went wheeling around his head. He stood in the bosom of thunder and the zig-zag lightning above him joined the muttering thunder . . . and Moses stood in the midst of it."[42]

All four identified elements of fiction work to strengthen the information the reader receives through the narrative and dialogue structures of the text. If he has not picked up the clues offered through linguistic structures, these elements by themselves convey to the reader the thematic intents of Hurston's fiction. But there is so much more insight available to the reader who looks attentively at language externally and internally and who recognizes that she has used the performances as well as the competencies of the language user to probe his consciousness and reveal the quality of his cultural possessions.

The following illustration offers further explanation of the conjunction or blend Hurston achieves between character and narrative voice in her literature.

In the samples that follow, each excerpted from *Their Eyes Were Watching God*,[43] I have selected portions of both dialogue and narration that illustrate the gradual movement of the blend. In the earliest samples, the narrative voice articulates the conceptual self-awareness that the characters lack at the beginning of the novels. Samples taken from the middle sections of the novel indicate the alternating voices of character and narrator. In these mid-sections, character and narrator often imitate each other's style. This midsection imitation is brief, and each voice quickly regains its distinctiveness.

In chapter 5 I discuss some of the structural and grammatical aspects that characterize the dialect. When narrative voice uses these structures it is an imitation of a style other than its own. The characters quoted in the midsections are beginning to gain insight into the personality of the flamboyant Jody Starks. They use the language of the dialect, adorned with both its poetry and grammatical distinctiveness, to assess the mayor's personality. These heavily adorned structures are usually reserved for moments of insight. Janie uses them on similar occasions. What should be noted here is that insight is an aspect of consciousness, more cognitive than performative. For that reason language that reveals consciousness is revealing an aspect of its spiritual being. It is the linguistic deep-structure that the dialect offers on the occasions when consciousness is probed. Because whatever insight the characters may have at the middle sections of the novel is temporary and brief, adorned language is limited in part two of *Eyes* as well as in Hurston's other novels.

We find the narrative voice of the last part of the novel enriched by the spiritual concepts gained from the dialect. And we find the dialect submerged into a fully adorned language that is capable of expressing knowledge of self and the insight into motivation and being that it has gained. The narrative language is now characteristic of dialect in both its structure and intent.

Samples of the narrative voices are as follows:

EARLY SECTIONS (in which the narrative voice articulates knowledge the characters lack about themselves).

Now, women forget all those things they want to remember, and remember everything they don't want to forget. The dream is the truth. They act and do things accordingly. (P. 5)

There are years that ask questions and years that answer. Janie had had no chance to know things, so she had to ask. Did marriage end the cosmic loneliness of the unmated? (P. 21)

Janie pulled back a long time because he [Jody] did not represent sun-up and pollen and blooming trees, but he spoke for far horizon. (P. 28)

MIDDLE SECTIONS (in which the characters begin to gain insight and narrative and character's voices may be interchangeable in dialectal structures and poetry).

Narrative voices:

A big-mouthed burst of laughter cut him short. (P. 38)

Joe would hustle her off inside the store to sell something. Look like he took pleasure in doing it. (P. 47)

Starks left the store to Hezekiah Potts, the delivery boy, and come took a seat in his high chair. (P. 57)

Daisy is walking a drum tune. You can almost hear it by looking at the way she walks. (P. 59)

She wasn't petal-open anymore with him. (P. 62)

Characters' voices:

Folkses, de sun is goin' down. De Sun-maker brings it up in de mornin', and de Sun-maker sends it tuh bed at night... let de light penetrate inside of yuh, and let it shine. (Pp. 40–41)

"You kin feel a switch in his hand when he's talkin' to you," Oscar Scott complained.
"He's uh whirlwind among breezes," Jeff Bruce threw in.
"Speakin' of winds, he's de wind and we'se de grass. We bend ever way he blows." (P. 44)

"Phoeby, for de longest time, Ah been feelin' dat somethin' set for still-bait. . . . Sorrow dogged by sorrow is in mah heart. . . . Ah'm stone-dead from standin' still and tryin' tuh smile." (P. 71)

FINAL SECTIONS (in which the narrative voice and the voices of characters are indistinguishable, their structure and poetry having blended into "poetic self-awareness").

Narrative voices:

Night was striding across nothingness with the whole round world in his hands. (P. 130)

The monstropolous beast had left his bed. The . . . wind had loosed his chains. He seized hold of his dikes and ran forward until he met the quarters; uprooted them like grass and rushed on. . . . The sea was walking the earth with a heavy heel. (P. 133)

And then again Him-with-the-square-toes [Death] had gone back to his house. He stood once more and again in his high flat house without sides to it and without a roof with his soulless sword standing upright in his hand. His pale white horse had galloped over waters, and thundered over land. The time of dying was over. (P. 138)

It was the meanest moment of eternity. . . . No hour is ever eternity, but it has its right to weep . . . the grief of outer darkness descended. (P. 152)

Characters' voices:

"If you kin see de light at daybreak, you don't keer if you die at dusk. It's so many people never seen de light at all. Ah wuz fumblin' around and God opened de door." (P. 131)

"Dis house ain't so absent of things. . . . It's full uh thoughts." (P. 158)

"And just listenin' tuh dat kind uh talk is jus' lak openin' yo' mouth and lettin' de moon shine down yo' throat. It's uh known fact, Phoeby, you got tuh go there tuh know there." (P. 159)

Because narrator and character speak with almost identical adornment in Hurston's final section of *Eyes*, there is little need for both voices to appear. This is the final test of the blend that has been achieved. In *Their Eyes Were Watching God*, narrator is the dominant, final voice. But we are certain at this point that the deep-structure consciousness of narrative voice and the deep-structure consciousness of character are identical. This is clearly illustrated when we find, in the final sentences of the novel, a voice that seems to be pure consciousness speaking. It is neither the direct dialogue of a character nor the objective commentary of the narrator who says: "Then Tea Cake came prancing around her where she was and the song of the sigh flew out of the window and lit in the top of the pine trees. Tea Cake, with the sun for a shawl. Of course he wasn't dead.... The kiss of his memory made pictures of love and light against the wall." (P. 159)

This voice brings the novel to closure. Janie is surrounded with imagery that is bright. Natural symbols like the pine tree point toward the universe. She is enclosed in the protective warmth of her home, and we understand that within its walls is a place that shines with her own awakening and is brightened by the poetry of her spirit.

NOTES

1. Janheinz Jahn, *Muntu* (New York: Grove Press, 1961), p. 124.

2. Henry Louis Gates, Jr., *Black Literature and Literary Theory* (New York: Methuen, 1984), p. 4.

3. Ibid., p. 5.

4. See John Szwed, "An Anthropological Dilemma: The Politics of Afro-American Culture," in *Reinventing Anthropology*, ed. C. Dell Hymes (New York: Vintage, 1974) for an overview of the anthropological perspectives that separated race and culture and led to the cultural deprivation/deficiency perspective.

5. Zora Neale Hurston, *Mules and Men* (Philadelphia: J. B. Lippincott, 1935; reprint, New York: Negro Universities Press, 1969; reprint, Bloomington: Indiana University Press, 1978), p. 3. (From Indiana Univ. Press ed.)

6. Wayne Booth, *The Rhetoric of Fiction* (Chicago: University of Chicago Press, 1961). Booth's discussion illustrates various narrative points of view for narrators who function within the text as either first-person characters or third-person commentators.

7. Ibid., pp. 149–209. I have abstracted the definitions for each category Booth addresses and formulated them into the structure of figure 2 (see p. 88). In this figure, Hurston's narrative system is compared to a traditional structure.

8. Although my personal preference is not to use the masculine pronoun in this context, to distinguish the narrative voices I discuss from the author's voice, I use *him* and *his* to avoid possible confusion.

9. Wilfred G. O. Cartey, "Africa of My Grandmother's Singing," in *Black*

African Voices, ed. James E. Miller et al. (Glenview, Ill.: Scott Foresman, 1970), p. 13.

10. Zora Neale Hurston, *Their Eyes Were Watching God* (1937; reprint, Greenwich, Conn.: Fawcett, 1969), p. 5.

11. Barbara Christian, *Black Feminist Criticism* (New York: Pergamon Press, 1985), p. 51.

12. Robert Hemenway, *Zora Neale Hurston: A Literary Biography* (Urbana: University of Illinois Press, 1977), p. 196.

13. Zora Neale Hurston, *Jonah's Gourd Vine* (1934; reprint, Philadelphia: J. B. Lippincott, 1971), p. 197.

14. Hemenway, *Zora Neale Hurston*, p. 196.

15. Hurston, *Jonah*, p. 198.

16. Hurston, *Eyes*, p. 13.

17. Hemenway, *Zora Neale Hurston*, p. 236.

18. Hurston, *Eyes*, p. 58.

19. Ibid.

20. Zora Neale Hurston, *Moses, Man of the Mountain* (1939; reprint, Urbana: University of Illinois Press, 1984), p. 144.

21. Hurston, *Jonah*, p. 19.

22. Zora Neale Hurston, *Seraph on the Suwannee* (New York: Charles Scribner's Sons, 1948), p. 4.

23. Hurston, *Jonah*, p. 224.

24. Hurston, *Moses*, p. 348.

25. Hurston, *Eyes*, p. 158.

26. Hurston, *Jonah*, p. 267.

27. Zora Neale Hurston to James Weldon Johnson, April 16, 1934, James Weldon Johnson Memorial Collection, Beinecke Rare Book and Manuscript Collection, Yale University Library.

28. Hemenway, *Zora Neale Hurston*, p. 200.

29. Hurston, *Moses*, pp. 344, 345.

30. Hurston, *Seraph*, p. 309.

31. Hurston, *Moses*, p. 64.

32. Ibid., pp. 31, 32.

33. Ibid., p. 111.

34. Hurston, *Eyes*, p. 131.

35. Hurston, *Moses*, p. 251.

36. Linguistic interference happens when speakers who are bilingual or bidialectal experience "cross-over" from the primary dialect when speaking a second. It is an incident of code-switching and often is attached to situations that are emotionally charged. Uriel Weinreich in *Languages in Contact* (The Hague: Mouton, 1963) has an important chapter on this phenomenon.

37. Hurston, *Eyes*, pp. 68, 69.

38. Hurston, *Jonah*, pp. 271–281.

39. C. C. Lovelace, "The Sermon," as recorded by Hurston in *Negro: An Anthology*, ed. Nancy Cunard (New York: Frederick Ungar, 1934), pp. 35–39.

40. Walter C. Daniel, *Images of the Preacher in Afro-American Literature* (Washington, D.C.: University Press of America, 1980), pp. 99–109.

41. Hurston, *Eyes*, p. 159.

42. Hurston, *Moses*, p. 351.

43. All citations are from the Fawcett edition of *Their Eyes Were Watching God*.

5

The Word, Thus Adorned, Bodies Forth Itself

I see, feel, and hear a potential celebration as African colors—thorough, direct. A thing of shout but of African quietness, too. . . . A clean-throated singing. Drums. . . . Costumery . . . a right richness that the body deserves.

—Gwendolyn Brooks, "The Field of the Fever, the Time of the Tall Walkers"[1]

The stark, trimmed phrases of the Occident seem too bare for the voluptuous child of the sun, hence the adornment. It rises out of the same impulse as the wearing of jewelry and the making of sculpture—the urge to adorn.

—Hurston, in Nancy Cunard, *Negro*[2]

Aspects of black language that inform literary deep structures help to develop an understanding of how the dialectal structures in Hurston's literature work to illustrate characters' developing awareness of themselves. This chapter offers a linguistic explication of the literary judgments made previously.

LINGUISTIC STRUCTURES

Much of the dialect study in the United States has concentrated on illustrating what people actually say and has paid less attention to the more informative but conceptually more abstract matter of what people know as they speak. This latter area of inquiry involves matters of linguistic competence, knowledge of the systems of language that are reflected in speech. To reveal those systems, study of linguistic deep-structure is necessary. Dialectology offers especially valuable information about the kinds of underlying structures that account for oral language differences in linguistic deep-structure. Cultural anthropologists have already laid a framework for this type of study. They insist that language is one manifestation of culture. Psycholinguists have shifted their cognitive concerns into areas of linguistic investigation, noting that the "most obvious thing we can say about the significance of a sentence is that it is not given as the linear sum of the significance of the words that comprise it."[3] Better understanding of dialects will come with study that concerns not only spoken surface-levels of language, but study of the areas of reference and meaning—the deeper levels of speech that determine surface variations. The underlying features of language may not be apparent in speech performances, but they are significant to competence and valid indicators of speakers' meaning and intent.

Transformational and generative grammarians' approach to deep structure as an information-laden area appropriately underscores the necessity of investigation at these levels of language. Deep-structure investigation establishes lexical and conceptual frameworks that interpret speakers' meanings. The listener who does not share these features, but who does understand the surface or performance categories of the language, will therefore receive only a portion of the original message; the rest is lost in "translation." Dialectal versions of a language offer themselves as material for investigating the deep structure of the variations as well as the reasons for their existence. Those aspects of the variations that are cultural and social, structures that linguistic anthropologists like Hurston and Boas took great pains to record, offer insights into meanings that are implicit among speakers of the dialect.

The black dialect falls very easily into such an investigative structure. Historically, it is a version of English that was mixed with various languages of West Africa and with French and Creole influences encountered along the slave-trading routes of this hemisphere.[4] Culturally, it has operated as a sociolinguistic boundary separating these speakers from speakers of standard English in America. The consequence of this separation has been the preservation of a certain cultural world view that could well have been lost had the black culture been more thoroughly integrated into America's mainstream. The survival of the dialect for more than a hundred years is testimony to the contemporary vitality of such systems of separation.

As a science, linguistic study is an accepted mode of statement concerning the nature and structure of communication. But what allows this scientific study to be a literary tool? Early linguistic science first applied itself to reconstructive and comparative studies of Indo-European languages. Linguistic study of culture and thought has shifted this descriptive emphasis to areas of cognitive psychology and sociology. These areas present additional information concerning language behaviors and knowledge within cultures, and, further, they suggest that literary investigations are a means of describing this knowledge of man "in" society. The liaison of natural and human sciences, framing the link between cognitive and behavioral patterns in man, functions as the basis for any language assumptions in these chapters. The sciences cannot be stratified; the link is vital.

Transformational-generative models of grammar account for both the knowledge of language and the performance of language skills within their theoretical structures. Although explanatorily adequate theories that completely explain the impetus behind the speech act have not yet been offered by linguists or psychologists, the attempt to account for these phenomena is an area of research receiving critical and important attention by these scholars. Through transformational grammar, linguists explain the operant processes of making and sharing memory and experience. Investigations of these processes reveal a conceptual model of the linguistic structuring of behavior,[5] and the area of dialectology is fertile ground for this type of investigation. Understanding that a people differ culturally and that there are linguistic differences between people who share the same geographic space suggests the importance of examining dialectal differences for information about the extent and kind of cultural distinctions separating these groups linguistically. Although the surface structure is where such study should be initiated, investigation must proceed to the levels of deep structure where speakers' meanings are represented within the deep-structure lexicon and transformational choices.

Methodology

To support the method I use to explain the role of grammar in the dialect of Hurston's literature, the following assumptions are offered in a "literary" analysis of her texts.[6]

The Priority of the Phonic Element. It is important to assert the oral origins of the black dialect, especially as we look at its evolution into literary structures. Because of its oral history, the written representation of the phonic intent is important. It is the phonic element that indicates that a difference from the standard structure exists. It is clear that Hurston was aware of this difference because her texts not only note dialogue with the traditional markers, but include dialogue written as "eye" dialect. Both the activity and the sound of speech were important to her. As we interpret her texts, we must take into account her effort to record speech that represented not only activity but sound. Insight into her texts occurs when we find a parallel between dialectal surface structures in her print and deep-structure characterizations.

Distribution and Functional Load. It is helpful to look at the linguistic appearance of certain aspects of the dialect from the perspective of "distribution," a term that "is applied to the range of contexts in which a linguistic unit occurs insofar as that range of contexts can be brought within the scope of a systematic statement of the restrictions determining the occurrence of the unit in question."[7] Because Hurston's literature fluctuates between standard and dialect usage, the element of distribution is especially important to the literary statement the dialectal structures make. If there is distribution of feature or structure, then this distribution determines what kinds of literary conclusions are available from this linguistic clue.

The appearance of dialectal features presents the opportunity to analyze their functional load. If the dialect were consistent in Hurston, less could be said about this feature. However, the language in her texts fluctuates between dialect and standard usage, and this flux sets up the potential for an intralinguistic contrast. Not only is intralanguage distribution important to distinguish voices in the text, but intralinguistic function becomes an important investigative element.

For both distribution and functional load, frequency determines whether or not that structure or feature merits its application to textual analysis. I have used "character type" and "situation" as restrictions that determine frequency.

Character type: If the element is used consistently by a character in Hurston who meets a "restrictive" classification, then its distribution is considered an aspect of characterization.

Situation: If the element is used consistently in situations that depend, at least in part, on linguistic "posturing," then additional analysis is indicated. These situations may be further stratified by determining whether they are (a) character provoked, (b) narrator provoked, or (c) provoked by some external event or force.

The validity and informational capability of a linguistic unit is determined by its frequency and the "informational content of a particular unit is defined as a function of its probability."[8] Probability and informational content are inversely related; that is, the greater the probability concerning a particular unit, the less information the receiver of that unit would lose if it did not occur. High probability predicts high redundancy. Therefore, in the analysis that follows, items in Hurston's texts that are less predictable are higher in informational content.

Finally, to illustrate the kind of literary explication of text that Hurston's complex interests and knowledge demand, I have analyzed the informational content of some selected features within her texts. Such a process illustrates the potential for using information theory as a method of literary criticism. Attention to the text in this way is but one response to contemporary demands within a black literary tradition for

> sustenance and for growth, the sorts of reading which it is the especial province of the literary critic to render; ... [to] share a fundamental concern with the nature and functions of figurative language as manifested in specific texts.... We can never lose sight of the fact that a text is not a fixed "thing" but a rhetorical structure which functions in response to a complex set of rules.[9]

Much of what Hurston says concerning the black dialect occurs only incidentally in her writings. She discusses briefly, in various communications to Hughes, some of what she has found concerning "some laws in dialect. Aspirate 'H' in certain positions."[10] Also, in Nancy Cunard's *Negro*, Hurston addresses the subject of dialect, noting again her findings about the aspirate *h* and saying that she can mention "only the most general rules in dialect because there are so many quirks that belong only to certain localities that nothing less than a volume would be adequate."[11] But when writing about information she would label "cultural," Hurston does tell more about what she sees in black dialectal patterns and characteristics:

> The primitive man exchanges descriptive words. His terms are all close fitting. Frequently the Negro, even with detached words in his vocabulary—not

evolved in him but transplanted on his tongue . . . must add action to it to make it do. So we have "chop-axe" "sitting-chair" "cook-pot" and the like because the speaker has in his mind the picture of the object in use. Action. Everything illustrated.[12]

Hurston continues her observation about the morphology of black speech by saying that the "Negro's greatest contribution to the language is (1) the use of metaphor and simile; (2) the use of the double-descriptive; [and] (3) the use of verbal-nouns."[13] She offers several examples of these categories, including the following for metaphor and simile:

You sho is propaganda
Sobbing hearted.
Kyting along.
Syndicating—gossiping
To put yo'self on de ladder

and double-descriptives like the following:

high-tall
little-tee-ninchy
low-down
kill dead
de watch wall

Her lists of verbal-nouns include these examples:

funeralize
She features somebody I know.
Sense me into it.
I wouldn't friend with her.
Uglying away.

Hurston notes that the "urge to adorn" is the impetus behind these phrases. Her decision to include items like these in the dialogue of her novels and stories emphasizes her intent to capture something of the character of the speaker as well as to tell his story.

My analysis of literary intent through the "spy-glass" of linguistic structures identifies two grammatical structures of the black dialect that have no equivalent in standard English. In addition, I have taken the clue from Hurston's observations in *Negro* and have chosen to illustrate examples from the categories of verbal-nouns, double-descriptives, and metaphors and similes for further literary explication. They are idiomatic in many situations, and, as a result, their meanings lie in their speakers' deep-structure lexicon rather than in a summary of the surface words that comprise them. Hurston uses idiomatic descriptors as adornment for language that cannot be rendered fully enough in either the standard or the traditional literary adornments of narrative language.

My final purpose is to illustrate a method of inquiry that is possible with dialectal investigation. Examples are taken from two novels, *Their Eyes Were Watching God* and *Jonah's Gourd Vine*, and the folk stories from *Mules and Men*.[14]

Items studied for potential literary interpretation may include any and/or all of the features identified as "1 to 4" in this chapter. My primary analytical consideration is that the higher the frequency of a feature, the less informational content is revealed. However, features that appeared in addition to another feature are assigned a greater informational value. For example, a language sample that included both features 1 and 4 from the listing is a higher informational sample than one that simply includes feature 4.

Features 1 to 4 include the following criteria:

1. *The language may be dialect*: Because the structural differences between narrative voice and the voices of Hurston's black characters are so clear, it is sufficient to define dialect as the language patterns within Hurston's fiction that differ in structure and sound from the narrative voice and the voices of the nonblack characters. The distinction of sound may be assumed when the graphemic representation of a dialectal item differs from the standard. For example, "Ah" is morphologically equivalent to the standard first-person singular pronoun "I," but the graphemic representation and its use by a black character indicate that it is an aspect of the dialect.

2. *The language may include an aphorism*: Aphorisms are deep-structure exchanges of information between speaker and hearer. Aphorisms may not be semantically explicit to nonspeakers of the dialect. An example of an aphorism is "God don't eat okra."

3. *The language may include metaphor, simile, double-descriptives or verbal-nouns, those elements Hurston described as the "urge to adorn."* The

inclusion of the items Hurston mentions in her contribution to the Cunard text is important for this analysis. They serve as the standard for defining the very dialectal items she thought important indicators of the culture of her characters. If the above are "adornments," then it is important to decide why this urge is a part of the characterization or situation Hurston has created. Some of the fullest expressions of these categories come within the black sermon. Hurston uses the same explanatory footnote in *Jonah* and *Mules and Men* in reference to the sermons she includes in these texts. She wrote that "In his cooler passages the colored preacher attempts to achieve what to him is grammatical correctness, but as he warms up, he goes natural."[15]

Hurston makes an important comment here, and has illustrated her notion of its importance by adding certain dialectal marks to emphasize the idea of adornment. Often she eliminates the grammatical features of the dialect one would expect in these situations as a means of highlighting the adorned language. This grammatical stripping serves her literary purposes as well as her academic. Adorned language marks a degree of intensity that the character, text or situation demands. At some points in her texts, the narrator's usually standard English is marked with adorned dialectal imagery. This generally occurs as the narrative voice blends with the dialectal voice of the protagonist, a situation discussed in the previous chapter. The blend takes place, not through structural or syntactic sharing, but through the sharing of the adorned language that has been saved for the emotionally intense exchanges or when character and narrator reach a common ground of awareness.

The following examples from *Their Eyes Were Watching God* indicate the sharing that occurs between character and narrator when awareness is achieved. In this novel, Janie expresses her love for Tea Cake in a philosophical reflection on the quality of their life: "We been tuhgether round two years. If you kin see de light at daybreak, you don't keer if you die at dusk. It's so many people never seen de light at all. Ah wuz fumblin' round and God opened de door."[16] The narrator matches the poetry of her adorned language in saying: "By morning Gabriel was playing the deep tones in the center of the drum. So when Janie looked out of her door she saw the drifting mists gathered in the west—that cloud field of the sky—to arm themselves with thunder and march forth against the world. Louder and higher and lower and wider the sound and motion spread, mounting, sinking, darking."[17] In the final pages, the narrative tone and style match the tone and style of Janie, who has come full circle and knows she has reached that pinnacle of life fully felt and fully known: " 'Ah done been tuh de horizon and back and now ah kin set heah in mah house and live by comparisons. ... Dey gointuh make 'miration 'cause mah love didn't work lak they love.... Then you must tell 'em dat love is lak de sea. It's uh movin' thing... and it's different with every shore.' "[18] The narrative assessment is: "The light in her hand was like a spark of sun-stuff washing her face in fire.... The kiss of his memory made pictures of love and light against the wall. Here was peace. She pulled in her horizon... from the waist of the world and draped it over her shoulder.... She called in her soul to come and see."[19]

Because the framework of the short story is quite different from the novel, we do not find the same structure of blend between narrator and character in the short story form. But the method is analogous. The narrative structure of the short story alters itself so that it can include different structures under the following situations: (1) to report a character's voice, (2) to comment in a narrator's voice and (3) to blend the narrator's knowledge with the character's thought and action. The result is that the character in situation 1 could say "Well, Ah done de bes Ah could. If things aint right, Gawd knows taint mah fault." The early narrative voice uses a third-person perspective in its commentary 2. "She sped to the darkness of the yard, slamming the door after her before she thought to set down the lamp." The final blending structure 3 of the narrative voice will allow a structure like this one, which seems consciously to avoid the use of persona: "Hours of this. A period of introspection, a space of retrospection, then a mixture of both. Out of this awful calm."[20] The structure is similar to a stream of consciousness, a textual structure suggesting the internal monologue that that method emphasizes.

Further examples of character adornments, lifted from relevant structures in *Their Eyes Were Watching God*, indicate the kinds of structures Hurston outlined in *Negro*:

—An envious heart makes a treacherous ear.

—Us colored folks is branches without roots.

—They's a lost ball in high grass.

—She... left her wintertime wid me.

—Ah wanted yuh to pick from a higher bush.

—You got uh willin' mind, but youse too light behind.

—he's de wind and we'se de grass.

—He was a man wid salt in him.

—still-bait

—big-bellies

—gentlemanfied man

—cemetary-dead

—black-dark

Within the structure of the sermon, this adorned language is abundant. The following examples are from *Jonah's Gourd Vine* and *Mules and Men*:

—I can see him—/Molding de world out of thought.

—when y'all is passin' nations thew yo' mouf.

—I am the teeth of time/That comprehended de dust of de earth.

—Faith hasn't got no eyes, but she long-legged.

—and de white capts marbilized themselves like an army and walked out like soldiers goin' to battle

—I can see-eee-ee/De mountains fall to their rocky knees

—And then de sacrificial energy penetrated de mighty strata

—Two thousand years have went by on their rusty ankles

—And de sun . . . laid down in de cradle of eternity/And rocked herself to sleep and slumber.

Neither in the sermon nor in actual dialogue is linguistic adornment a common factor—making the informational content of these occurrences relatively higher than the occurrences of dialectal structures without the adornment. It is a much less speculative task to assign various cultural interpretations to these occasions than it is to speculate about the more subtle grammatical forms. We have additional information on the culture through the various traditional structures of fiction that are, of course, an important aspect in Hurston's text. The adornment present in the dialect on selected occasions is not unlike the adornment given to literature as a genre. It has traditionally been a "loftier" language, commonly associated with the language of poetry. Hurston, in a previously quoted letter to James Weldon Johnson, said that the Negro preacher was a poet, one who "manipulates words in order to convey to others the mystery of that Unknowable force which we call God."[21] The parallel is appropriate: she has found occasions when the dialect is poetry as it conveys self in an intimate spiritual sense. When the preacher gets warmer he uses more dialect. With the heightening of emotional exchange, adornment increases. When the narrative structure gets closest to the aspect of character that reveals spiritual self-knowledge and awareness, adornment increases. These parallels cannot be accidental for an author who not only noted the existence of these features but whose novels extended those structures into characterization.

4. *The language may include the lexical items "done" or "be" to express features in the auxiliary system of the deep structure.* I have chosen to focus on the auxiliary system within the dialect's deep structure because that system explains the syntactic behavior of words and elements in the surface structure. Meaning differences within the auxiliary systems are related to time, a concept that investigative evidence in anthropological linguistics supports as culturally specific. Studies in the black dialect[22] suggest that correlations may be made between categories of time within the black dialect and some Creole dialects. Although there have not been definitive studies of comparisons of the dialect to West African languages or forms of English, the historical connection of black American dialects to the Caribbean Islands and West Africa makes the association between these languages and cultures both historically accurate and linguistically sound.

An analysis of *done* shows its occurrence within the black dialect under the circumstances illustrated in figure 2. In addition, *be,* like *done,* occurs in environments in the black dialect that have no equivalent auxiliary structures in standard English.

The difference between the dialect and the standard in Hurston's texts' dialogue should be investigated through the historical perspective of language variations and change and/or cultural foundations where cultural distinctions have mandated such differences. If we had more specific information regarding the African origins of the dialect, the latter distinction might be easier to identify. But, because research in this area is unfinished, only the following speculations seem appropriate.

FIGURE 2
Black Dialectal and Standard English Surface Structures and Their Representative Auxiliary Components Governing *Do* and *Be* Deletion and Insertion

		AUXILIARY	
	BLACK DIALECT	DEEP STRUCTURE	STANDARD ENGLISH
2.1	done took	<+perfect>	have taken
2.2	been took	<+passive> <+perfect>	have been taken
2.3	done been took	<+passive> <+perfect> <+intensive>	0
2.4	she lookin	<+progressive>	she is looking
2.5	she be lookin	<+progressive> <+durative>	0
2.6	she do be lookin	<+progressive> <+durative> <+intensive>	0

a. When *done* signals intensity (feature 2.3), the auxiliary carries the intensive marker in addition to the progressive or perfect aspect. Its semantic inequivalence to *have* or *has* is displayed in structures like 2.1 (that are frequent in Hurston's fiction and therefore informationally insignificant). In these structures (like 2.1), intensity is not implicit and therefore is not present as an auxiliary component.
b. Note that structure 2.6 has generated *do* in response to the <+intensive> marker and uses the present-tense form.
c. Feature 2.5 *be* appears when the durative marker is on an auxiliary. Its semantic inequivalence to *is* is displayed in structures like 2.4 (that are frequent in Hurston's fiction and therefore informationally insignificant). In these structures (like 2.4), duration is not implied as an auxiliary marker and the copula *be* is deleted from the surface structure in the black dialect. When *be* appears in the surface structure, its lexical-feature list will include the durative marker.

First, because information theory tells us that the frequency of an item is inversely related to its informational value, it is reasonable to assume that the surface-structure differences in items that are, in the deep structure, lexically equivalent to standard English structures (2.1, 2.2 and 2.4), are not informationally significant items.

Second, because features that have no standard English equivalents (2.3, 2.5 and 2.6) have a low frequency of appearance in her texts and are therefore significant, these features call for literary analysis of character and situation.

Finally, because in some situations *done* appears in the black dialect where it cannot be generated in the standard, some attention is necessary to the lexical list representing this structure to determine whether the morphology of these items is indeed culture-specific.

Transformational-generative theory asserts that speakers' knowledge "of the idiosyncratic properties of words may be represented as a kind of internalized dictionary . . . a lexicon."[23] The idiosyncracies of language represented by the lexicon come from the way a language is learned and internalized along with the world views specific to its culture. The selectional restrictions on language use within that culture express the cultural choices. Within the black culture, a more significant statement must be made because, instead of dealing with language differences between cultures, we face dialect differences. Therefore, only the areas of significant distinction between the dialect and the standard language are appropriate areas to investigate for differences that may be culturally provoked.

Structural differences such as the syntactic distinctions between standard English and the black dialect use of the feature call for a look at the deep-structure lexicon to approach the understanding the dialect conveys when selecting this structure.

It is particularly important in the analysis of the feature to incorporate the use of a lexicon because standard English eliminates this feature in the surface structures in almost all the environments where the black dialect retains it. In addition, the dialect carries lexical environments that have no parallel in the standard. The lexical information the black dialect maintains through its representation of *done* in the surface structure, carries the concept of intensity.

5. *The language may be standard usage of English within the structure of the adorned narrative voice.* The inclusion of this feature allows analysis of the structures in Hurston that blend the voice of the narrator and

the voice of character as described in chapter 4. Analysis within a linguistic framework explains these appearances of adorned language that had been assigned to the dialect in the narrative voice. Under circumstances in which the distinction between the structures of narration and the dialectal structures of dialogue diminish, adorned language may be interpreted as an occurrence of the special, loftier language usually reserved for literature. Within the perspectives of the analyses I have suggested, it is also possible to see the author's creation of what amounts to a third point-of-view. The blend of the dialectal and narrative structures forms a point-of-view that supplements those of the narrator and characters.

In view of their frequency and distribution, two categories of items meet the criteria of significance in information theory. They are: (1) the syntactic structures listed in figure 2 as 2.3, 2.5 and 2.6, and (2) the morphologic descriptors included in the aphorism, the sermon and the blending structures of the narrative voice. The following literary interpretations explicate the environments surrounding these features with reference to the specifications of situation and character described earlier. Because the basic structure of Hurston's novels is different from her folk stories and short stories, these two forms of fiction will receive separate analysis. However, one of the results of this linguistic analysis of literary structures in Hurston indicates that the structure of the short fiction and her folk stories abbreviates the narrative structure of the novel in a way that suggests that the same authorial intent, to use these structures to give a clearer view of character, was present in both.

Literary Explication and Analysis. The syntactic structures that create comments like "Ah'm done give out" and "he bes sick" appear in these novels in especially dramatic or emotional situations. Janie is exhausted after fleeing the rushing waters of the lake that is flooding its banks, threatening the folk of the surrounding area. She, Tea Cake and Motor Boat try to warn others as they run past shanties in the water's path. Finally, they reach high ground and she declares that she can make it no further. "Ah'm done give out," she exclaims. Tea Cake replies to her, "All of us is done give out." Their exhaustion, fear and confusion are mirrored in the intensive structure in their voices. *Done* reflects that lexical intensity to the structure and notes the dialect's syntactic response to a category of meaning its users deem important as they express their realities.

The semantic construct of this structure can best be explained by a comment that Janie's grandmother makes to her in *Their Eyes Were Watching God.* She tells her granddaughter that "Ah ain't gittin' ole, honey. Ah'm done ole." It is clear that she is speaking of a category of time. But further than that, it is a category that suggests her intensity in a way that a standard English "I am old" could not suggest. For this reason, *done* notes the lexical presence of this emotion.

This dialect has also found it necessary to include a semantic construct that suggests a distinction between times when something is done habitually and times when something is done occasionally.[24] When Lucy tells her daughter Isis in *Jonah's Gourd Vine* not to let the women "be covering up de clock" when she dies, she is indicating a performance she anticipates because it is a habitual practice within her culture.[25] A person unaware of the mythic backgrounds of this activity would not understand the implication of the text. But attention to the linguistic clue found in the use of *be* offers at least the suspicion of significant deep-structure lexical information attached to that string.

Neither of these structures, the intense *done* or the durative *be*, appears frequently in her fiction. When they do appear, the clue to meaning is contextual. Hurston often translates dialectal items or offers some explanation for the behavior of her characters in footnote references. The fact that she felt this necessary indicates her awareness that the language held culture-specific information that may not have been accessible to all her reading audience.

Sop's final pronouncement regarding his friend Tea Cake summarizes both plot and theme in *Their Eyes Were Watching God.* After Tea Cake's death, Sop says that he "had done gone crazy"—using the intensive category to express his sense of the extreme reaction of his friend to the debilitating effects of rabies and his notion of the completeness of Tea Cake's insanity. This included taking a woman seventeen years his junior as a lover. In Sop's eyes, what had happened to his friend was intensely overwhelming and tragic. We are privy to the level of his consciousness through the revealing structures in his dialect. Had Hurston not used the category of intensity at this point in the text, the breadth of the sentiment would not have been as impressive.

In addition to information from syntactic structures, the morphologic structures of these texts also present clues for analysis of character and situation found in descriptive categories within the dialect and the narration.

Of course, it is true that all literature describes through the images of its vocabulary. But what happens with the dialect and with the narrator's linguistic association with the dialect are those same ideas of adornment Hurston had explained in *Negro*. For the narrators of her folk stories who are speakers of the black dialect, even literary language was an aspect of the "stark, trimmed phrases of the Occident." This is an observation that Hurston utilizes when the narrator changes his commentative structure at those points of text that mark the blending narrative. Hurston asserts through the blend that there is more room within the semantic and syntactic constructs of the dialect for such illustration, that the dialect is better able to picture the experience. The construct uses double-descriptives, verbal-nouns and a wealth of poetic tools to underscore spiritual experiences. The language of both characters and narrator becomes nearly metaphysical when the sermon is introduced in *Jonah*. Because in this novel the character never attains the level of self-awareness that the narrative voice enunciates for him, only the temporary medium of the sermon is capable of expressing his spiritual depths. John recognizes the power of the narrative voice in his statement that it is not his "self" but the voice of God speaking through him when he sermonizes. The blend we should expect in the final pages of the novel between John's voice and the narration doesn't occur. Instead, the narrative language blends with the spiritually inspired voice of the sermon.

> And the preacher preached a barbaric requiem poem. On the pale white horse of Death. On the cold icy hands of Death. On the golden streets of glory. On Amen Avenue. On Halleluyah Street. On the delight of God when such as John appeared among the singers about His throne. On the weeping sun and moon. On Death who gives a cloak to the man who walked with a feeling of terrible loss. They beat upon the O-go-doe, the ancient drum. O-go-doe, O-go-doe, O-go-doe! Their hearts turned to fire and their shin-bones leaped unknowing to the drum . . . the voice of Death—that promises nothing, that speaks with tears only, and of the past.[26]

This structure, apparent at the end of the text, not only suggests that the measure of truth is found in the blend of ancestral spirit with Christianity, but it also serves to explicate an earlier segment of text. In the early portion language celebrating the end of cotton picking uses African imagery. "They danced," the narration explains, "They called for the instrument that they had brought to America in their skins—the drum—and they played upon it. It was said, 'He will serve us better if we bring him from Africa naked and thingless.' " A traditional literary analysis at this point of the novel would offer two possibilities: (1) that "He" is, as the text suggests, the white man speaking of the African, Cuffy, or (2) that "He" could be something different. At this early juncture in *Jonah*, any alternatives to possibility 1 are moot. However, with the knowledge that the blending narrative provides at the text's end—that there is reason and truth lying between the African celebration and this newly Christianized soul—the passage has far greater potential. The black African, who has retained his self-knowledge, reasons that his god ("He") could serve him better if he did not cloak him with some other religion. The final message of the book is that had John been true to his spirit as well as to his flesh, he could have survived. As it was, his loss of an African truth was tantamount to a loss of his soul.

Within the structures of the folk stories of *Mules and Men*, the literary functions of these syntactic structures become evident partly because the abbreviated form of folk stories allows such literary signals to play a more important role. It is also because, in this text, the narrators of the stories are real people, speakers of the dialect themselves. For the speakers, a significant part of the construction of these stories is to separate the voices in the stories from their own voices. This effort produces even further evidence of the literary functions of language structures in the telling and interpreting of story.

The "adorned" structures, simile, metaphor, double-descriptives and verbal-nouns, are abundant in Hurston's folktales. The folk story structure presents a special opportunity to use the adorned form of language. The narrative entry into stories in *Mules and Men* often begins with a Muselike evocation similar to this one from the collection: "Ah got to say a piece of litery fust to git mah wind on," an announcement that is followed by a recitation of poetry to warm up the speaker for the storytelling that follows. The equivalent to something like "once upon a time" concedes control to the word that follows and becomes in the dialect "Let me talk some chat," or, "Hurry up an plough up some literary." Characters in these stories speak such soliloquies as this one: "Old Maker, wid de mawnin' stars glitterin in you shinin crown, wid de dust from yo footsteps makin worlds upon worlds, wid de blazin bird we call de sun fling out of yo right hand in de mawnin and consumin all day de flesh and blood of stump-black darkness."[27] In examples such as these, personification, simile and metaphor abound. It is significant that the most poetic dialect in the folk stories is found within the stories that have a religious theme. This form of story and the language within it are similar to the sermon form, discussed earlier, that also relies on abundantly poetic/adorned language. It is as if the spiritual topic demands a language that can accommodate it.

But that language is not restricted to the storytelling. Talking about telling a story can provoke language structures as dramatic as the language structures of the story itself. "Let de dollars hush whilst de nickel speak," says one adult to another, trying to clear the way for a youngster to tell a story. Storytelling can provoke a competitive spirit leading the participants to challenge the descriptive capacities of the language:

> "Man, he's too ugly. If a spell of sickness ever tried to slip up on him, he'd skeer it. . . . "
>
> "He ain't so ugly. Ah seen a man so ugly till he could get behind a jimson weed and hatch monkies."
>
> "Ah knowed one so ugly till you could throw him in the Mississippi River and skim ugly for six months."
>
> "Ah knowed dat same man. He didn't die—he jus' uglied away."[28]

In *Mules and Men*, Lennie Barnes speaks with the full inflection and syntactic markers of the dialect as long as he is outside of the storytelling structure. "Lemme handle a li'l language long here" he says, about to enter the role of storyteller. "Y'all ever hear 'bout dat nigger dat found a gold watch?"[29] His shift to storyteller is accomplished by a "bit of literary" unrelated to the story itself but a critical device to indicate his shift from a man who can tell stories to a narrator. After his "entry" is spoken, "Well, once upon a time was a good ole time / Monkey chew tobacco and spit white lime," the narrative voice, barely marked by dialectal structures, emerges: "A colored man was walking down de road one day and he found a gold watch." Once the narrative voice is established, the dialect can emerge again, as a character who says at the tale's end, "It's a quarter past leben and kickin' lak hell for twelve." Even though some marks of dialect are present in the dialogue, the black character's speech is marked by the adornment of personification—Hurston's indication that it is within the structures of the black dialect that the potential for the adorned word is realized. The important element within the storytelling environment is that within the black culture storytelling encourages such a consciousness of language that the creative urge almost spontaneously adorns the language.

Hurston indicates through the language and the storytellers' consciousness of language that they are the story as well as the tellers of story. Hemenway speculates in his biography of Hurston that she chose the form for *Mules and Men* because of a need to illustrate the stories she had gathered for her sponsors and also because of a need to illustrate the origins of these stories. They could not have been presented outside of the cultural setting because the adornment of the language within the stories was the adornment of the storytellers themselves. These phrases are by no means as apparent in her longer fiction, in which Hurston had a chance to present the perspective of a nonparticipant-narrator. Within the structures of the short fiction there is no nonparticipation. The storytellers have a stake in the story to the extent that when it is over, they are so caught up in the act of linguistic creation that they need cooling down just as they needed the literary warm-ups. They end with structures like: "Biddy, biddy, bend—my story is end. Turn loose de rooster and hold de hen."[30]

Adorned language within the black dialect furnishes an identification of another level of consciousness. It is *nommo*—a self-consciousness of creative potential. Most language has so distanced itself from its creative genesis that it is a level of consciousness no longer accessible. It is certainly not equivalent to a standard narrative structure because it compels involvement of narrator and audience in the content of the fiction and reflects the choral character of the word, echoing the call-and-response traditions of black spirituality. It is this involvement and participation that distinguishes Hurston's use of dialect in her fiction. No other forms demand an eventual merging of character and narrator, a linguistic blend that highlights the understanding and/or resolution. No other forms demand an audience participation that creates a sermon between preacher and congregation, rather than a sermon from preacher to congregation. The aspect shared between speaker and listener was created from the structures of the language that connected a group of speakers in a positive way—an African community that the systems of slavery and racism in this country have sought to eradicate.

The creative word was like Morrison's protective ancestor, the spirit that watched over, protected and communicated the cultural legacy of its people.

The syntactic environments of *done* (see figure 2) in the short stories and folktales add to the examples present in the longer literature and reinforce the assumptions concerning the semantic categories. Its use suggests an intensity not possible with the simple past and not equivalent to the standard English perfect tense. This is illustrated in structures that permit the standard English *had* in the perfect aspect of "dat mosquito had done cleaned up ten acres" and also *done* in the perfect aspect of "Ah done dropped my hammer" (figure 2, feature 2.1, note a). *Had* and *done* cannot both be perfect. The dialect indicates, again, that the form carries an additional lexical marker. *Done* acts as an intensifier when it appears in addition to the perfective or progressive features. It is as if the speaker must indicate that no matter what accoutrements of the standard he uses, his own dialect's cultural markers must be included for the semantic sense he want to convey. His reality governs the linguistic community in his words. He communicates more than grammatical structure—he communicates cultural sense. His responsibility to his audience is to forward that message. Hurston's responsibility to her audience is to make us aware that the potential exists.

When the reader approaches text from this linguistic perspective, understanding the potential for the structure of the dialect to carry such messages as intensity and finality, a more accurate appraisal of literary structures like characterization is possible. Awareness of the aspects of the dialect that adorn language further strengthens the critical perspective. The link between a syntactic structure such as *do* and the more semantic aspects of adornment is fundamental to language. They comprise two of its most basic elements: syntax and morphology—order and sense. Cued to Hurston's texts by features that recognize phonological variations, an "eye-dialect," these features work to increase our cognitive awareness of the language user. Variations in structure can provide subtle nuances in meaning. Because aspects of meaning are culturally determined, then elements of language that inform "sense" can give the informed listener or reader far more information.

When, in the conversation near the saw mill in *Mules and Men*, the men discover they need not have reported for work that day, Black

Baby says, "We coulda *done* been gone." Hurston has italicized the *done*. The reader who is prepared to make a linguistic judgment on this dialectal structure would know, even without Hurston's emphasis, that Black Baby is frustrated and angry with someone. For the many times when similar structures appear that are not italicized, the additional insights into the character's consciousness are available to readers clued to look to dialectal structures for textual explication.

John Pearson understands his mother's focus on his father's habitual drunkenness when she says "he be's drunk when he keer on lak dat." John acknowledges this understanding in his retort: "I don't keer if he do be." The reader who understands this exchange will not only be able to see something more of his father's character than is sketched in the short space this book devotes to him, but can make a better appraisal of John's reaction in addition to developing background information concerning the characters who will frame the protagonist's life. Dialect can help to fill in information, to speculate on authorial intent, and to further clarify the critical judgments we make concerning literature.

Finally, we learn how dialect can accomplish for language what poetry accomplishes for prose. In the same manner that a line of poetry loses force, beauty and its concise construction and imagery when translated into prose, dialect loses those qualities when translated into the standard. Dialect and poetry both intensify. Their adornment and special structures are their speakers' conscious manipulations of language to render their experiences as they have felt them. It is a mimetic act—an effort to re-create, through the word, the experiences of a culture. An informed and critical reading audience must be aware of the effort as well as willing to give close enough scrutiny to the text itself to interpret the message of an author such as Hurston, who has specialized her language through the structures, the sounds and the sense of her dialect.

NOTES

1. Gwendolyn Brooks, "The Field of the Fever, the Time of the Tall Walkers," in *Black Women Writers*, ed. Mari Evans (New York: Doubleday, 1984), p. 78.

2. Zora Neale Hurston, "Characteristics of Negro Expression," in *Negro: An Anthology*, ed. Nancy Cunard (New York: Frederick Ungar, 1934), p. 31.

3. George Miller, "Some Preliminaries to Psycholinguistics," in *Psycholinguistics and Reading*, ed. Frank Smith (New York: Holt, Rinehart and Winston, 1973), pp. 16, 17.

4. See J. L. Dillard, *Black English: Its History and Usage in the United States* (New York: Random House, 1972) for a discussion of the historical backgrounds of the dialect.

5. It is important to note that the discussion of deep-structure transformations as they generate surface-structure performances are *conceptualizations* of the shifts that meanings experience as they become linguistic. Although transformational complexity as it reflects a surface-structure complexity may be represented through the grammatical theory in my discussion, this theory is one of many conceptualizations of competence/performance grammatical models. Here, the transformational-generative grammer reflects the research of theorist Noam Chomsky, *Syntactic Structures* (The Hague: Mouton, 1957).

6. The theoretical structure of my discussion in this chapter is based on notions of frequency and distribution and functional load in John Lyons, *Introduction to Theoretical Linguistics* (Cambridge, England: University Printing House, 1958), pp. 81–93.

7. Ibid., pp. 70–71.

8. Ibid.

9. Henry Louis Gates, Jr., "Criticism in the Jungle," in *Black Literature and Literary Theory*, ed. Gates (New York: Methuen, 1984), p. 5.

10. Zora Neale Hurston to Langston Hughes, James Weldon Johnson Memorial Collection, Beinecke Rare Book and Manuscript Collection, Yale University Library. In her discussion on this subject, Hurston wrote of "some laws in dialect. The same form is not always used. Some syllables and words are long before or after certain words and short in the same position. Example: 'you' as subject gets full value but is shortened to 'yuh' as object. 'Him' in certain positions and ' 'im' in other depending on consonant preceding. Several laws of aspirate 'H.' " The tone of this letter supports the scholarly interpretation of Hurston's awareness of dialectology.

11. Hurston, "Characteristics of Negro Expression," p. 31.

12. Ibid., p. 24.

13. Ibid., p. 25.

14. I selected these texts for analysis because they contain many kinds of dialect usage and the characterizations and narrative structures vary widely within individual stories as well as in each text.

15. Zora Neale Hurston, *Jonah's Gourd Vine* (1934; reprint, Philadelphia: J. B. Lippincott, 1971), p. 316.

16. Zora Neale Hurston, *Their Eyes Were Watching God* (1937; reprint, Greenwich, Conn.: Fawcett, 1969), p. 131.

17. Ibid., pp. 129–130.

18. Ibid., p. 158.

19. Ibid., p. 159.

20. Hurston, "Sweat," *Fire!!* 1 (November 1926), pp. 40–45.

21. Hurston to James Weldon Johnson, April 16, 1934, James Weldon Johnson Collection, Yale University Library.

22. Dillard in *Black English* writes that the durative *be* and perfective markers *done* and *been* signal remote and immediate aspects according to his analysis. He draws a parallel between these aspects to WesKos Pidgin English of Nigeria and the Cameroons.

23. Roderick Jacobs and Peter Rosenbaum, *English Transformational Grammar* (Lexington, Ky.: Xerox Publishing, 1968), p. 59.

24. This feature is referred to as the "durative" *be.*

25. The myth surrounding this incident refers to the fear that the newly released soul will be captured in the mirror by its glance.

26. Hurston, *Jonah*, pp. 311–312.

27. Zora Neale Hurston, *Mules and Men* (Philadelphia: J. B. Lippincott, 1935; reprint, New York: Negro Universities Press, 1969; reprint, Bloomington: Indiana University Press, 1978), p. 50. (From Negro Universities Press ed.)

28. Ibid., p. 94.

29. Ibid., pp. 115, 116.

30. Ibid., pp. 54, 132.

6

The Spiritual Legacy in the Word

> Dance and Drums preceded the word. . . . Magic/Religion came before "criticism," and words (nommo) were the rappings of not one but thousands of Spirits. Centuries before the "literary capitals" of London, Paris, and New York, Ife, in Nigeria, was the home of the Necromancers, heavier than Solomon, conjurers of dread and joy. Kidnapped by bandits to North America, they became HooDoo men, maintaining the faith of the old religion.
>
> —Ishmael Reed, "Can a Metronome Know the Thunder or Summon a God?"[1]

Ishmael Reed described "Necromancers of two worlds . . . "speaking in tongues" as neo-Hoodooism, an acknowledgment of the shards of black religions that were maintained through the traditions of the literary word—a tradition Hurston searched out at its most primary source.

What kinds of motivations pushed Hurston's literary talents toward a celebration of her people through their linguistic creativity? *Their Eyes Were Watching God*, a masterful stroke of literary complexity, is an acknowledgment of the African traditions that nurtured black American fiction. It came as a harbinger announcing a writer capable of sustaining literary complexity through the vehicle of linguistic structures. In this one novel, Hurston caresses the natural imagery and beauty of the verdant South, struggles with the forces of human will complemented and contradicted by nature; outlines the situation of a mulatta whose heroine status, unlike her predecessors in the tragic mulatta tradition, arises not from her color but from her will and out of her community; and asserts the beauty of language and imagery in black Southern dialect that carries the vision and nuances of an insular community. This novel was a point of literary genesis that Hurston conceived in the pages of *Jonah's Gourd Vine* through the mystic and spiritual depths that her language scoured. But the necessary period of its incubation for the complexities of *Eyes* came during the research that eventually spawned her two nonfiction works and her growing respect for the community that sustained the word; this despite sociopolitical realities in the Americas. After the period of gestation, her powerful novels *Eyes* and *Moses* almost birthed themselves. But it is important to look carefully at her research, her academic biases and the published structures of her field work to understand the creative and spiritual lineage of these literary efforts.

I believe that *Mules and Men* and *Tell My Horse*, the research that founded them, the scholarship that produced them, and the literary eye that crafted them are the true sources for Hurston's view of language as creator. Their publication assured that the research that consumed Hurston through her early professional years would find a voice both accessible to her people and representative of her skill. Had she assumed the traditional role of social/linguistic scientist, the beauty of the word would be masked in the trappings of academe, but it was to her credit that Hurston felt secure enough in her blackness not to mask her language in this way. Her possessive awareness combined with her academic scholarship and research in forages through the black Southern communities of the United States, the Caribbean Islands and Haiti to structure a research perspective that would be a catalyst to the creation of her literary word. Through her investigations of the primal black communities of the Americas, those whose links to the motherland were least culturally diffused by the slavers, she was assured that the source of the culture she celebrated was truly African. The language through which she colored the characters of her celebrants led her to its idea as she traveled through the Caribbean communities. Her research there assured the birthing of the creative word, the message in the linguistic and literary structures discussed in earlier chapters. A researcher who looked at "behavior" as an indicator of "thought," she was prompted to probe areas of consciousness and culture to account for the survival of African mythologies in the communities of these areas. She was to learn that through Hoodoo, the spirit of Africa was given flesh; Hoodoo enabled a physical and visual survival of the religions of the mother continent.

Hurston's goal was to provide an insider's view of Hoodoo, not an anthropological study like Herskovits's *Life in a Haitian Valley*, a work that Hurston noted as definitive on the culture of this island. Her effort was to understand "the contradictions inherent in Haitian culture in the 1930s"[2] and to present the dynamics of racial, cultural and gender conflicts alongside a view of the practices of voodoo. It was a religion—a term Hurston understood as being significant to understanding its structure. Her representations of the practice always included its basic spirituality and never bowed to the Christian portrayal of Hoodoo as a heathen practice lacking anything of spiritual value or definition. Part of the Christian difficulty with Hoodoo was that its Western manifestation was cloaked in Catholicism,[3] an irony Hurston did not fail to note and had used earlier as the thematic base of *Jonah's Gourd Vine*.[4] In her research, she observes that the survival of Hoodoo on the Caribbean Islands documents a culture's insistent hold onto the practices and beliefs that had defined it in Africa. Recognizing the relative insignificance of its alliance with Christianity in the face of the deeper spiritual values that were represented by Hoodoo's survival, her discussion of "Voodoo and Voodoo Gods" in *Tell My Horse* spends little time with the Catholic manifestations of the gods. Instead, Hurston begins with the more important review of the African/Haitian cosmology of the religion. She writes, "in the logic of one who practices and believes"[5] of the schema of the religion, concentrating on the gods and goddesses as the source of the beliefs and the power of their survival.

I believe it was especially significant to Hurston to present Hoodoo as a religion that offers a schema for creation and life that began, like the Judeo-Christian religions, with the assertive power of the word. However, for Hoodoo, this creative act, *nommo*, was a six-day period during which God uttered magic spells and incantations, a complexity of linguistic activity that fit a religion described in *Muntu* as a "hierarchical body of priests, a community of believers, temples, altars, ceremonies and finally *an oral tradition* [emphasis added]."[6] *Moses* uses a great deal of the creation theology for its text and gathers its strength around the magicalness of the word. We can see this impetus for a literary rendering of her research in the second half of *Mules and Men*, where the opening discussion of Hoodoo is a presentation of the creation story. In *Tell My Horse* this theology is repeated with the naturally fertile and sensual symbology of the Caribbean Islands as their backdrop. Hurston explains that the Catholic imagery in the rituals is due to French colonialism, but focuses our attention on the survival of the blackness of the myth. She notes that the pictures of Catholic saints included in the practice are not Afro-Haitian gods in "whiteface," but approximations of the Haitian gods (*loa*). Because the linguistic mythology was primal, Hurston explains in these texts, the visual rendering of the imagery was less significant than the word itself.

As a survivor of the middle passage, Hoodoo is an example of the persistence of a culture through the ravages of slavery and sociopolitical diffusion in the Americas. When Hurston wrote of Jamaican blacks that they "are beginning to respect themselves . . . to love their own things like their songs, their Anansi stories and proverbs and dances,"[7] she was writing of the African selves that were respected in spite of the pervasive problems of color in that community—the "triadic relationships of the mulatto Jamaican male, his self-assured light-skinned wife . . . and the deceived brown-skinned rural maiden."[8] Although the issues of color and class (caste) did not assume major proportions in these works, Hurston underscored her interest in this issue through her literary rendering of the mulatta in the novel published between *Mules and Men* and *Tell My Horse* (Janie in *Their Eyes Were Watching God*). Later, in an essay titled "How It Feels to Be Colored Me," she wrote that she was not "tragically colored."[9]

It is important to note in Hurston's essays on the Caribbean the development of the methods of "formalized curiosity." This methodology, personalized through her own vision of the word, her people and her developing literary talents, would direct investigations initiated by her academic mentor, Franz Boas. Hurston was selective during these occasions, as she had been earlier. She made clear choices as to which perspectives of Boas she would carry with her. She copied his methodology and accepted his view that the primary tool of the researcher was a command of the language of the community to be studied, that it was an "indispensible means of obtaining accurate and thorough knowledge."[10] Her early error in research, bringing her "carefully accented Barnardese" to her field work, highlights the special nature of her linguistic anthropology. She was, as her professor demanded, in command of the language of the community, but not as an outsider. She not only knew the language, it was her primary dialect, and as such her native language. Had she chosen the option, her native speaker's knowledge as well as her "Barnardese" could have rendered that knowledge in standard research format and style. Although the glamour of Barnard and its standard English was the source of failure for her first field work, it also underscored for Hurston the issue Boas highlighted in his *Handbook of American Indian Languages*[11]—that knowing and using the language of the "informant" is an important adjunct to a full understanding of the customs and beliefs of the people under study. Hurston took this one step further. She was a native speaker of the communities she would investigate in the United States. She accepted the need to learn the Creole dialect to use as an entry into the cultures of the Caribbean. Therefore she held a linguistic as well as cultural identity with and empathy for the "informants" and accepted a responsibility to celebrate their cultures through her double vision. It is because of her vision and belonging that Hurston parted company with standard methods of reporting field-research data and chose a literary vehicle for presenting the bulk of her data. She could not offer her findings as scientific statement—such a form would not only negate the value of her participation but would be only the scientific "surface structure" of such information. This superficial descriptive reporting was characteristic of linguistic research and statement in the 1920s and 1930s. Hurston had to assert the depths of her own research by selecting a presentation that would testify to her knowledge and the accuracy of her data. It was not, as Mikell suggests, a "conflict" that prompted Hurston to make such a choice. Mikell writes: "One senses within Hurston's work an inherent conflict which derives from the fact of her blackness: an identification with the people she studies, and a willingness to participate in their reality, as well as an intellectual separation from them but a reluctant pronunciation of judgment and characterization."[12]

It is also important to note that there is a significant and critical connection between the final form of *Mules and Men* and the structure of her novels. Hemenway describes the connection as answering her "scholarly problem . . . her responsibility . . . [and] stance" as she made "others see this great cultural wealth."[13] Not only does this research stand as testimony to her people's cultural beauty, but it formed for Hurston the basis for structuring the African notion of *nommo* into her literature. She had made tentative steps in this direction with *Jonah*. But her first novel was restricted in its intimate association between the word and its spiritual source. The complexity of the novels written after the research experiences clarified for her the expansive, creative potential of the word. Rather than experiencing difficulty or conflict with the role she acknowledged as both subjective and objective, Hurston wrote with satisfaction of the "spy-glass" of anthropology that allowed her to stand off and look at the "garment" of her memories, things she had not been able to see because they "fit [her] like a tight chemise."[14] Her schooling gave her the equipment to perform that "dissociation of sensibility" that Hemenway writes of as characteristic of her fiction, and it is a distancing that Hurston celebrates rather than sees as a conflict. Her choice to document the word, the actual statements of people in the midst of the social and political changes in the Caribbean, was a decision to let their words speak her judgments. Their words are unambiguous indictments of Western colonialism and the tragic results of Western values, represented by the white man, his color and his material goods, superceding cultural preservation. When she quotes the Haitian peasant who looks forward to the American occupation of Haiti because the "black man is so cruel to his own,"[15] she indicts not the black culture but the Western oppression that has caused such intracultural conflict. Her presentation of the anthropology of these islands was unanticipated because she wrote in the voices of both participant and observer. But the judgments we expect from the cultural anthropologist are lacking. Instead, she selects voices from those she had interviewed to illustrate the complexity of these islands and her own voice professes no pretensions at knowing "what is wise and best." We do know what Hurston felt because the full and colorful pictures of her research rendered literary speak for her. It is to her credit that she managed to avoid, for the most part, the intrusive voice of the scientist and that she acknowledged the power of the word to define its own history and construct its own prophecies through her literary imaging of its character, its nature.

Boas's influence is seen throughout Hurston's linguistic renderings of her texts when, for example, she translates a phrase such as "rockatone at ribber bottom no know sun bot" in *Tell My Horse* to "the person in easy circumstances cannot appreciate the sufferings of the poor." Her careful avoidance of a word-for-word linguistic transformation illustrates Boas's principle that for poetry, which for Hurston was the "adorned" dialect, "no translation can possibly be considered as an adequate substitute for the original. The form of rhythm, the treatment of the language, the adjustment of the text to music, the imagery, the use of metaphors . . . can only be interpreted by the investigator who has equal command of the ethnological traits of the people and their language."[16]

Hurston noted in *Tell My Horse* that in preparation for entering any gatherings from which she might elicit information, she was very careful to learn the Creole dialect of the Caribbean Islands. She was readily able to acquire this dialect because of the relatively short historical reality of either black English or the Creole because their linguistic point-of-origin was identical.[17] I suspect her sensitivity was not only due to her training, but to her cultural understanding that she had to belong to a community before its people would share their intimacies with her. Although she forgot this for a brief period, testing as it were the inadequacies of the Euro-American access to black culture,[18] she remembered it in time to make the significant contribution to research in Hoodoo and black folklore in *Tell My Horse* and *Mules and Men.*

Each of Hurston's regional expeditions, the first to America's South and the second to the Caribbean, is linked to the other through the shared historical and cultural features of the black communities. The link that Hurston explored in greatest detail was Hoodoo. Her interest lay in its spiritual expression of the ceremonies and mysticisms of West African religion.[19]

In New Orleans, Hoodoo was called "sympathetic magic" and practiced by "two-headed doctors." In the Caribbean community, closer to African linguistic patterns than the African-American communities, blacks remained faithful to the African pronunciation of the Dahomeyan term *vudu.*[20] Hurston noted the conflict between the initial consonants in Voodoo and Hoodoo, and, though she used them interchangeably in her texts, she notes that whites in America pronounce the term with the *v* that is faithful to the African pronunciation and that Blacks have replaced the initial consonant with an aspirate *h.*

Although she explores the Caribbean forms of Hoodoo in one text, and American Hoodoo in the other, noting that New Orleans is the "Hoodoo capital of America," there are occasions when Hurston compares the practices of the two areas in an effort to establish that the cultural relationships between blacks happens even when dispersion is the operant sociopolitical factor. The phenomena of God-in-nature and the in-dwelling god is an ancient and African theology. Its appearance in the communities Hurston investigated, in the form of Hoodoo, furnishes an important element in establishing the cultural connections between blacks in this hemisphere. It was mostly accident that the ritual and symbolism of the Catholic church became involved in this worship. The ornate trappings of Catholicism appealed to the African's "urge to adorn," and the networks of saints in this religion was a convenient vehicle in which to store the multitude of spirits that inhabited the African view of the world. The *loa* became more visual through their appearance as the Catholic saints, but Hurston cautions her readers to recognize that the change was not in their natures, merely in their features. Gathering information and sharing the visual imagery and ceremonial significance of Hoodoo, Hurston offers a culturally enlightening vision of a spiritual aspect of an African-American's world view.

In both of her texts on Hoodoo, Hurston follows her established pattern as a teller of folktales as well as introducer of some of the sociopolitical implications of Western colonialism. It is a "speakerly text"[21] in this regard—telling its tale on its own without the dominating value judgments of a narrative voice.

Her descriptions of the rituals of the Caribbean islands (birth, death and marriage) highlight the important linguistic elements in these ceremonies. The special section devoted to the position of women in the Caribbean clearly illustrates her attention to feminist issues. Although the latter issue was not a major thesis in these works, and she may have, as Mikell suggests, "shifted to the level of the outsider in order to grasp the richness of cultural data in Jamaica," the status of women in these islands was portrayed by Hurston with "delight, intrigue and outrage."[22] Her feminist perspective emerges more appropriately in her literature through her character Janie. Here again is a case of Hurston finding literary outlet for her social research.

Both texts make their greatest contribution through their sociological perspectives enriched by the narrator-as-participant structure rather than as a detailing of the intense and specific rituals involved in Voodoo worship. Worth noting in her construction of *Mules and Men* and *Tell My Horse* are her criteria for selection of significant cultural and historical issues and her organization of the data. It includes an appendix that functions as a glossary, a sampling of folk songs, prescriptions from famous root doctors and worship songs of Hoodoo.

Her major basis for including material seems to be whether or not she had a personal experience that verified the data given her in inquiry concerning the Hoodoo community. For four months in New Orleans, she asked questions and received answers but "nothing was put on paper," a respectful and informed acknowledgment of the important tradition of oracy in this culture and the power of the spoken word to direct its own truth. She followed a similar method in the Caribbean, and it was not until her questions directed her toward a primary source did she allow her words to engage a text. This is an important illustration of her insistence that the word be traceable to a valid source, unadulterated by the tradition of its passage through various channels. Her insistence is further clarified by her use of first-person narration. This style distinguishes her experiences and conversations as a participant in Hoodoo ceremonies from others' experiences and tellings of their tales. Her contributions as narrator-participant are rendered without the marks of the dialect that her speakers used. This structure helps us understand the authenticity of the text, and we are thus privy to a much more personal view of Hoodoo. The cures, potions and spells she and her teacher prepare for others are recorded in the style of her folktales. In this manner she tells not only the methods the doctors employ in various situations, but also the stories that surround the informants. By using such an approach, she offers her own form of the informants' double vision—how they manage the mechanics of their worship and how it affects them. To reinforce the effectiveness of her texts, she includes in *Mules and Men* a section labeled "Conjure Stories" that illustrates the attitudes of the black community toward sympathetic magicians. Such a presentation of her research covers all possible perspectives, and the picture we are left with is one that vibrates with the liveliness of these communities.

The texts *Mules and Men* and *Tell My Horse* have a parallel structuring. Each of their sections on Hoodoo begins with a historical survey of the areas in which it has been practiced. In *Mules and Men* this survey's emphasis is on giving the origins of Hoodoo "the way we tell it." Testimony, presented in the form of conversation between two neighbors, follows the survey, and her discussion of points-of-origin is again left to the words of those most directly involved. She has acknowledged the scientific requisite of validating data through the same approach that piques a nonscientific audience's interest in reading the absorbing narrative of the traditions she researched.

Tell My Horse is a much longer and more detailed text than the published result of her research in New Orleans, but opens with a similar historical survey and political perspectives of Jamaica and Haiti. Her organization reflects an investigation into Hoodoo that respects the mythology of the islands and traces the African sources of the worship. A narrative detachment that was evident in *Mules and Men* also follows her discussions in *Tell My Horse.* And it is significant that this detachment is most evident when she has involved herself as a participant in the rituals she describes. Both books couple her own experiences with the larger topics of the origins and practices of Hoodoo. The network that joins these topics is established first by a discussion (in *Mules and Men*) of the history of Hoodoo priestess Marie Leveau and her kin who were Hurston's first teachers. Their lessons led to contacts with clients. The contact with clients leads the reader to a larger chapter of conjure stories, told by those clients who had come to her for cures. The network in *Tell My Horse* is similar, but has an additional element. The members of the community who inform her concerning Hoodoo also give her the opportunity to reflect on the effects of colonialism within the culture of those islands.

These were texts that anticipated black nationalism thirty years before it found its way to the Americas. But in a more intimate sense, these are texts that illustrate the developing of Hurston's awareness of the magic in the words that were part of her memory. More than being vehicles to illustrate a positive cultural experience, they could themselves reconstruct the experience as they livened the communities that America threatened with neglect. We can also apply to Hurston what Christian writes of Morrison's novels, that

> we are first introduced in these novels to the place that the characters inhabit, the land of the community. Like the ancestral African tradition, place is as important as the human actors, for the land is a participant in the maintenance of the folk tradition. It is one of the necessary constants through which the folk dramatize the meaning of life, as it is passed on from one generation to the next.[23]

Hurston was truly a necromancer—speaking and thereby giving life to a tradition that Morrison would discover as primal ground in her contemporary novels. In those forages into spiritual places that sustained those African traditions, Hurston learned, consumed and finally shared with her readers those places through her literary and linguistic artistry. In *Moses*, that ground was a rock; in *Their Eyes Were Watching God*, that ground was fertile earth that grew its own communities. In *Seraph*, that ground was a swampy reminder of the mired values of white America. Important in all her work past those treks across ground that held black spirituality was the potential of the black word to "know the thunder" and "summon [its] gods."

NOTES

1. Ishmael Reed, "Can a Metronome Know the Thunder or Summon a God?" in *The Black Aesthetic*, ed. Addison Gayle, Jr. (Garden City, N.Y.: Anchor Books, 1972), p. 318.
2. Gwendolyn Mikell, "When Horses Talk: Reflections on Zora Neale Hurston's Haitian Anthropology," *Phylon* XLIII, no. 3 (September 1982), p. 225.
3. Hurston notes this cloak, and removes it as she attends to the African backgrounds of this religion.
4. See the discussion in chapter 2 of this book.
5. Mikell, p. 226.
6. Janheinz Jahn, *Muntu* (New York: Grove Press, 1961), p. 33.
7. Zora Neale Hurston, *Tell My Horse: Voodoo Gods, An Inquiry* (Philadelphia: J. B. Lippincott, 1938), p. 20.
8. Mikell, p. 223.
9. Zora Neale Hurston, "How It Feels to Be Colored Me," *World Tomorrow* 11 (May 1928), p. 215.
10. Franz Boas, "Linguistics and Ethnology," in *Language in Culture and Society*, ed. C. Dell Hymes (New York: Harper and Row, 1964), pp. 15–22.
11. Ibid.
12. Mikell, p. 222.
13. Robert Hemenway, *Zora Neale Hurston: A Literary Biography* (Urbana: University of Illinois Press, 1977), p. 159.
14. Zora Neale Hurston, *Mules and Men* (Philadelphia: J. B. Lippincott, 1935; reprint, Negro Universities Press, 1969; reprint, Bloomington: Indiana University Press, 1978), p. 3. (From Indiana Univ. Press ed.)
15. Hurston, *Tell My Horse*, p. 23.
16. Boas, pp. 15–22.
17. Both dialects are extensions of West African parent languages.
18. Her first attempts were failures. She wrote in *Dust Tracks* that she carried too much of the Barnard culture with her and failed to trust her own background within the black community.

19. Hurston is always very careful to note that Hoodoo is a "religion," a spiritual worship system. In learning the ceremonies and rituals of the religion, she underscores the importance of this perspective of Hoodoo.

20. The Dahomeyan pronunciation (*vudu*) is significant because the port of departure in Dahomey for many slave ships was "Ouidah," a place-name used today in Hoodoo ritual. The major Hoodoo god is "Damballah Ouedo." Hurston notes many names of Rada deities that are Dahomeyan place-names in *Tell My Horse.*

21. Gates's term for this book is used in his chapter "The Blackness of Blackness: A Critique of the Sign and the Signifying Monkey" in *Black Literature and Literary Theory*, ed. Gates (New York: Methuen, 1984).

22. Mikell, p. 224.

23. Barbara Christian, *Black Feminist Criticism* (New York: Pergamon Press, 1985), p. 48.

Conclusion

My conclusion, like Hurston's voice, is recursive. It begins, it names, it activates, it calls us back to a primal ground.

In several languages of West Africa, creation myths include the presence of a drum that beats life into existence. In these myths, God uses a drum as his word—in turn it becomes an instrument of procreative power. With such mythology collected from its past, the word of contemporary black cultures, African and African-American, contains in its cultural subconsciousness the imaginative and figurative symbology of this legacy. Does such consciousness touch the levels of reality? Barfield would argue that the poet, as a maker of meaning, has the specific task of preserving myths—the theocratic earliest meanings, "natural expressions of man's being and consciousness" and "*given*, as it were, by Nature . . . they could not be *known*, but only experienced or lived."[1] Once we separate ourselves from that archaic expression, once our language evidences a distance between self and Nature, then the level of meaning that is symbolic and mythic can only be retrieved and remembered through metaphor. This is the realm of the poet, and this is the creative place of Hurston.

Place was important to Zora Neale Hurston—she would spend most of her adult life in search of a place that she could claim as her own—one that would support, with fervor equal to hers, her cultural nationalism, that would respect the legacies represented in the voices that she recorded—voices that evidenced the traditions of the word.

Recently, I heard Zora Neale Hurston's voice for the first time. On the tape, she was singing and explaining how she learned the folk tunes that she had heard during her collecting trips. She had the "map of Florida" on her tongue, and it was a magical moment for me, hearing the voice of the woman whose literary voices had haunted and stroked and sensitized me like the incantations they were, readying me to explore the imaginative depths in the black dialect. Her voice was no less imaginative; and more clearly than I could have imagined, it indicated as the source of its song the culture that carefully and craftily and oftentimes surreptitiously maintained the vestiges of its traditions. Within the dialect, in its sound, its structures and its meanings, the culture of a people is preserved and protected. Within the artistry of Hurston, this oral culture is rendered literate.

There is a powerful mind set to overcome here. Hurston was dealing with a dialect that even its black writers, like James Weldon Johnson and Paul Laurence Dunbar, felt was a "jingle in a broken tongue." She was preserving a language that linguists saw as an attempt at English, broken, or truncated, or otherwise disabled from full reflective and cognitive power. She was dealing with a reading audience who was willing and ready to laugh at the humor in their "exotic savages" and an audience who was black and interested in denying that anything other than songs sung "serenely sweet" evidenced their presence in America. She had a powerful myth to supercede. But Hurston never abandoned the poetry of her folk or the milieu that allowed her to express character deep down where it was evident what character was about, at the level of consciousness and thought.

As I have discussed throughout this volume, there are several ways to investigate the linkages in literature between language and character. Language points out, identifies and draws attention to character. Language defines and clarifies for that character, and, because it is part of a communicative system, it points out and defines this textual awareness for the reader as well. The critical concept in reading Hurston's texts for evidence of their allegiance to the black word is to read them for the new literary vision they craft and for the different critical posture they explore. Language and character are linked through the expertise and whim of the poet. When the poet works the literary word, she is playing her instrument. Like the drum of African mythology it is procreative and conceives a linguistic energy that leaves its creator behind as it generates complexities of awareness built on the sustaining, stable word. Hurston's fiction speaks of the primacy of the word, the instrumentation of literary talent and the metaphorical adornment of a culture that recaptures myth on its tongue and uses the adornment to represent itself as black.

Within the text, the affirmative power invested in this word is an affirmation of black self. Dialect carries the poetry of myth in its adorned structure, and when dialect and narrative voices merge to each carry poetry, they each celebrate the poetic artisan. Hurston, I feel, understood that she celebrated herself through her word, crafted herself, affirmed herself, and perhaps most important and most primal, *named* herself. She has brought back together the contemporary distinction between form and content, subject and object, by literalizing language as self and word as character. Giving spiritual substance to her characters through the subtle variations of language within their voices and the narrative voices, allowing them a participant-structure within the form of the fiction in terms of their growing into the textual narrative structures, was in a very real sense giving substance and form to her own "self." The "stance" she took relevant to her scholarship and research and talent was to deny that these were disciplines that could not be collapsed under the influence of her mighty talents.

Hurston chose language to be the constant in her multidimensioned self. This radical position flew in the face of the academic perspectives of her mentor and the social perspectives of an emergent black middle class. In her indication that black speech was not a separate "language," but a dialect that drew from its linguistic pasts the ideas and structures of the languages that contributed to its viability, Hurston contradicted the conceptualization of black language as an unsuccessful (due to the speaker's inability and the language capacity's smallness) attempt at mimicry of standard language patterns. In addition, the rationale for cultural deficiency, a postscript to this notion of mimicry and truncation, falls disabled as she uses dialect for the vehicle to express the complex consciousnesses of her people. Her note in *Negro* that the dialect appears and sustains itself because the language of the West has such sterility that it cannot contain the adorned consciousnesses of black folk is an affirmation of the linguistic power that she understands exists within this dialect. It is, as well, an affirmation of the power she saw in herself, a speaker of the dialect. As she crafted characters, she assured them their souls through the linguistic universe they carried with them, giving them spirits in the same manner she realized her own.

Her reminder to her reading audience was that language is a reliable mechanism to support and develop the cultural consciousness of her characters. What is remarkable about this reminder is that it was offered during a time when anthropological science was bent on indicating the lack of difference between cultures. It was a powerful school of thought to dispute, and any contradiction of this thinking was a reflection on her academic mentor, Franz Boas. Her folktales represented her recognition that the voices of her people would undergird their stories with the realities of their cultural experiences. As an artist who understood all the relevancies of language and culture, she gave her literature a power that could not ignore its linguistic implementation. Taking language into consideration meant she also had to think about what language meant to the user. Hemenway's introduction to *Mules and Men* (1978) quotes Ralph Ellison's observation that the folklore of black America was an "especially courageous expression," an announcement of "the Negro's willingness to trust his own experiences, his own sensibilities as to the definition of reality."[2] The reality of the language user and the reliability of his voice were essential to preserve in a culture that stripped him of his drum and robbed her of the voices of her generations.

The theory of voices that preserve a primal and generative word is a theory that works its way into Hurston's fiction, her stories of storytellers and her records of Hoodoo. "Belief in magic is older than writing," she wrote in *Mules and Men*. She writes of the old magicians, Moses and the Queen of Sheba, as a man and a woman who learned of the power in words. This wisdom of the "ancient times" is what "we talk again" in rituals of Hoodoo. Again and again Hurston warns her audience that the magic, the reality, the power and all "their flaming glory" lie in the words of her people. The characteristic diminishing of dialogue in Hurston's novels, when her characters' internal retreats are about to bring them in touch with their own souls, is an indication that Hurston believed that whoever uses language, the artisan-author or the character constructed by that author, must connect the self to the spiritual source of linguistic power. Consciousness of this power is different for her many kinds of characters. John Pearson senses the power in his words as the "voice of God talkin thru me." Janie recognizes the emptiness of Jody's brag as a lot of "big voice." His cohorts recognize this as well, "he's de wind," they say, but they note that Janie is "un born orator... [who can] put jus' de right words tuh our thoughts." Her task is to call this voice back to her own soul, to "call [it] back from its hiding place" and let it name her life for her. Moses' soul calls him. The figurative structures of his being a man who has "been called" by the voice of God are identical to the calling Janie finally attends to and John fails to learn from. Pitiful Arvay leans toward a voice but finds a cultural sterility that leaves her empty. Her best effort is to "listen to the light"—ever an external image for her because inside she is barren and soulless. She has no community to claim, a family she suspects she only decorates and serves from a distance and a culture that she has rejected.

Hurston's language, in form and substance, reinforced the telling narrative structures, the blending epiphanies, the loud silences of dialogue that foreshadow journey's end for the soul. Her novels are vitalized by their internal poetic structures, and, when these structures are shared with her characters, a final act of creation is accomplished. Hurston saw herself as the artisan and recognized the word as her material. As far as linguistic structures are concerned, there is no void between form and content—only the potential of the voice to blend, and, through its blending, to construct.

Zora Neale Hurston was archetype, adorned as her people and as full of the mythology of her Eatonville as the storytellers on Joe Clarke's porch steps. She knew this, and celebrated and flaunted her community—daring the world to contradict what was her reality. She was a marvelous collage, a vision of the collected wisdom of what it meant to be black and female and talented and sure of herself in a culture that would deny her any of these identities.

For literature to be mimesis, it must agree to face the mirror and acknowledge its reflection. After the glance within one can choose to replace masks. Janie did this after Jody Starks died. First she checked to assure herself that her spirit was intact, then she replaced the mask, covered herself again and "starched and ironed her face" for the outside world. She has not subverted the vitalizing of the soul. She has claimed it as hers to control.

Today, we are increasingly aware of Hurston's masks—shields that assured her some control of her own image. I would hope that we respect these masks and that we do not try to hard to remove them in our fervor to discover, for example, what happened in the ten years of her life we now know she hid in her autobiography. I would hope that we focus our creative efforts on assuring her the stature she deserves and that we respect this artisan-necromancer who could cover and recover the voices of a culture. The accumulated layers of her soul are lovingly and graciously represented in her regenerative words. When Zora Neale Hurston "ploughed up some literary," she retrieved for each of us the word from its ground and brought it back to re-create culture and sustain its myth in a recognition that the fundamental creative potential of the universe is a female and a linguistic principle. The range of her literature is testimony to the complexity, sufficiency and wholeness of her culture in an era that challenged such a definition.

NOTES

1. Owen Barfield, *Poetic Diction* (1928; reprint, Middletown, Conn.: Wesleyan University Press, 1973), p. 102.
2. Robert Hemenway, Introduction to *Mules and Men*, by Zora Neale Hurston (Bloomington: Indiana University Press, 1978), p. xxvii.

Bibliography

PRIMARY SOURCES: WRITINGS BY ZORA NEALE HURSTON

1. Books

Jonah's Gourd Vine. Philadelphia: J. B. Lippincott, 1934. Reprinted, with an introduction by Larry Neal, Philadelphia: J. B. Lippincott, 1971.

Mules and Men. Philadelphia: J. B. Lippincott, 1935. Reprinted, New York: Negro Universities Press, 1969. Reprinted, with an introduction by Robert Hemenway, Bloomington: Indiana University Press, 1978.

Their Eyes Were Watching God. Philadelphia: J. B. Lippincott, 1937. Reprinted, Greenwich, Conn.: Fawcett, 1969. Reprinted, Urbana: University of Illinois Press, 1978.

Tell My Horse: Voodoo Gods, An Inquiry. Philadelphia: J. B. Lippincott, 1938.

Moses, Man of the Mountain. Philadelphia: J. B. Lippincott, 1939. Reprinted, with an introduction by Blyden Jackson, Urbana: University of Illinois Press, 1984.

Dust Tracks on a Road. Philadelphia: J. B. Lippincott, 1942. Reprinted, with an introduction by Darwin Turner, New York: Arno Press, 1969. Reprinted, with an introduction by Larry Neal, New York: J. B. Lippincott, 1971. Reprinted (second edition), with an introduction by the editor, Robert Hemenway, Urbana: University of Illinois Press, 1984.

Seraph on the Suwannee. New York: Charles Scribner's Sons, 1948.

2. Other Publications

"Drenched in Light." *Opportunity* 2 (December 1924), 373–374.
"Spunk." *Opportunity* 3 (June 1925), 171–173.
"The Hue and Cry About Howard University." *Messenger* 7 (September 1925), 315–319, 338.
"Muttsy." *Opportunity* 3 (August 1926), 246–250.
"Possum or Pig." *Forum* 76 (September 1926), 465.
"The Eatonville Anthology." *Messenger* 8 (September, October, November 1926), 261–262, 297, 319, 332.
"Sweat." *Fire!!* (November 1926), 40–45.
"Color Struck: A Play." *Ebony and Topaz*. New York: National Urban League, 1927.
"Cudjo's Own Story about the Last African Slaver." *Journal of Negro History* 12 (October 1927), 648–664.
"How It Feels to Be Colored Me." *World Tomorrow* 11 (May 1928), 215–216.
"Dance Songs and Tales from the Bahamas." *Journal of American Folklore* 43 (July–September 1930), 317–418.
"Hoodoo in America." *Journal of American Folklore* 44 (October–December 1931), 317–418.
"The Gilded Six-Bits." *Story* 3 (August 1933), 60–70.
"Characteristics of Negro Expression." In *Negro: An Anthology*, ed. Nancy Cunard. New York: Frederick Ungar, 1934.
"Story in Harlem Slang." *American Mercury* 55 (July 1942), 84–86.
"High John de Conqueror." *American Mercury* 57 (October 1943), 450–458.
"The Last Slave Ship." *American Murcury* 58 (March 1944), 351–358.
"Crazy for this Democracy." *Negro Digest* 4 (December 1945), 45–48.
"Conscience of the Court." *Saturday Evening Post*, March 18, 1950, 22–23.
"What White Publishers Won't Print." *Negro Digest* 8 (April 1950), 85–89.
"I Saw Negro Votes Peddled." *American Legion Magazine* 49 (November 1950), 12, 13, 54–57, 59–60.
"A Negro Voter Sizes Up Taft." *Saturday Evening Post*, December 8, 1951, 29, 150.

3. Unpublished Materials

"Book of Harlem." Short story, 7 pp. James Weldon Johnson Memorial Collection, Beinecke Rare Book and Manuscript Library, Yale University Library.
"The Chick With One Hen." Character sketch, 2 pp. James Weldon Johnson Collection, Yale University Library.

"The Emperor Effaces Himself." Character sketch, 7 pp. James Weldon Johnson Collection, Yale University Library.

"Mule Bone: A Comedy of Negro Life." Play in three acts, written with Langston Hughes. Act 3 was published in *Drama Critique* (Spring 1964), 103–107. The authorship remains in litigation; only portions of it are available for public viewing at the Yale University Library.

4. Correspondence

Portions of letters referenced and directly quoted in my text that either concern Hurston or were written by her are a part of the James Weldon Johnson Memorial Collection, Beinecke Rare Book and Manuscript Library, at the Yale University Library.

SECONDARY SOURCES

Barfield, Owen. *Poetic Diction*. 1928. Reprint. Middletown, Conn.: Wesleyan University Press, 1973.

———. *Saving the Appearances: A Study in Idolatry*. New York: Harcourt, Brace and World, 1957.

———. *Speaker's Meaning*. Middletown, Conn.: Wesleyan University Press, 1967.

Barthes, Roland. *Elements of Semiology*. 1964. Reprint. Boston: Beacon Press, 1970.

———. *Writing Degree Zero*. 1953. Reprint. Boston: Beacon Press, 1970.

Bone, Robert. *The Negro Novel in America*. New Haven: Yale University Press, 1958.

Bontemps, Arna, ed. *The Harlem Renaissance Remembered*. New York: Dodd, Mead, 1972.

Booth, Wayne. *The Rhetoric of Fiction*. Chicago: University of Chicago Press, 1961.

"Boys 10 Accuse Zora." *Baltimore Afro-American* 11, October 23, 1948.

Brickell, Herschel. "A Woman Saved." *The Saturday Review of Literature*. November 6, 1948.

Brown, Sterling. *The American Negro: His History and His Literature*. New York: Arno Press, 1969.

Chomsky, Noam. *Syntactic Structures*. The Hague: Mouton, 1957.

Christian, Barbara. *Black Women Novelists*. Westport, Conn.: Greenwood Press, 1980.

———. *Black Feminist Criticism*. New York: Pergamon Press, 1985.

Cunard, Nancy, ed. *Negro: An Anthology*. New York: Frederick Ungar, 1934.

Daniel, Walter C. *Images of the Preacher in Afro-American Literature*. Washington, D.C.: University Press of America, 1980.

Dillard, J. L. *Black English: Its History and Usage in the United States*. New York: Random House, 1972.

Du Bois, W.E.B. *The Souls of Black Folk*. 1903. Reprint. New York: Fawcett Publications, 1961.

Dunbar, Paul Laurence. "An Ante-Bellum Sermon." *The Complete Poems of Paul Laurence Dunbar*. New York: Dodd, Mead, 1896, 1913.

Ellison, Ralph. "The World and the Jug." *Shadow and Act*. New York: Vintage Books, 1964.

Evans, Mari, ed. *Black Women Writers: A Critical Evaluation*. New York: Anchor Press/Doubleday, 1984.

Gates, Henry Louis, Jr. " 'A Negro Way of Saying.' " *New York Times Book Review*. April 21, 1985.

———, ed. *Black Literature and Literary Theory*. New York: Methuen, 1984.

Gayle, Addison, ed. *The Black Aesthetic*. New York: Anchor Press/Doubleday, 1972.

———. *The Way of the New World*. Garden City, N.Y.: Doubleday, 1976.

Gloster, Hugh. *Negro Voices in American Fiction*. New York: Russell and Russell, 1965.

Hemenway, Robert. *Zora Neale Hurston: A Literary Biography*. Urbana: University of Illinois Press, 1977.

Howard, Lillie P. *Zora Neale Hurston*. Boston: Twayne Publishers, 1980.

Hurst, Fannie. "Zora Neale Hurston: A Personality Sketch." *Yale University Library Gazette* 35 (1961).

Hymes, C. Dell. *Language in Culture and Society*. New York: Harper and Row, 1964.

———. *Reinventing Anthropology*. New York: Vintage, 1974.

Jacobs, Roderick, and Rosenbaum, Peter. *English Transformational Grammar*. Lexington, Ky.: Xerox Publishing, 1968.

Jahn, Janheinz. *Muntu*. 1958. Reprint. New York: Grove Press, 1961.

Jordan, June. "On Richard Wright and Zora Neale Hurston: Notes Toward a Balancing of Love and Hatred." *Black World* 23 (August 1974).

Lee, A. Robert, ed. *Black Fiction: New Studies in the Afro-American Novel Since 1945*. New York: Barnes and Noble, 1980.

Locke, Alain, ed. *The New Negro*, 1925. Reprint, New York: Collier Books, 1971.

———. "Jingo, Counter-Jingo and Us—Part 1. Retrospective Review (and Biography) of the Literature of the Negro: 1937." *Opportunity* 1 (January 1938).

Lyons, John. *Introduction to Theoretical Linguistics*. Cambridge, England: University Printing House, 1958.

Mbiti, John. *African Religions and Philosophy*. New York: Doubleday/Anchor, 1970.

———. *The Prayers of African Religion*. Maryknoll, N.Y.: Orbis Books, 1975.

Mikell, Gwendolyn. "When Horses Talk: Reflections on Zora Neale Hurston's Haitian Anthropology." *Phylon* XLIII, no. 3 (September 1982).

Miller, George. "Some Preliminaries to Psycholinguistics." *Psycholinguistics and Reading*. Ed. Frank Smith. New York: Holt, Rinehart and Winston, 1973.

Miller, James et al., eds. *Black African Voices*. Glenview, Ill.: Scott, Foresman, 1970.

Reed, Ishmael. "Can a Metronome Know the Thunder or Summon a God?" *The Black Aesthetic*. Ed. Addison Gayle, Jr. Garden City, N. Y.: Anchor Books, 1972.

Rodgers-Rose, La Frances, ed. *The Black Woman*. Beverly Hills: Sage Publications, 1980.

Schraufnagel, Noel. *From Apology to Protest: The Black American Novel*. Deland, Fla.: Everett/Edwards, 1973.

Singh, Amritjit. *The Novels of the Harlem Renaissance*. University Park: Pennsylvania State University Press, 1976.

Southerland, Ellease. "Zora Neale Hurston: The Novelist-Anthropologist's Life and Works." *Black World* 23, no. 10 (August 1974).

Staples, Robert. *The Black Woman in America: Sex, Marriage and the Family*. Chicago: Nelson-Hall Publishers, 1973.

Tate, Claudia, ed. *Black Women Writers at Work*. New York: Continuum, 1983.

Thurman, Wallace. *Infants of the Spring*. New York: Macauley, 1925.

Walker, Alice. "In Search of Our Mothers' Gardens." *Ms.* 2, no. 11 (May 1974).

———. "In Search of Zora Neale Hurston." *Ms.* 3, no. 9 (March 1975).

———, ed. *I Love Myself When I Am Laughing: A Zora Neale Hurston Reader*. Westbury, N.Y.: The Feminist Press, 1979.

Washington, Mary Helen. "Black Women Image Makers." *Black World* 23, no. 10 (August 1974).

Weinreich, Uriel. *Languages in Contact*. The Hague: Mouton, 1963.

Index

About the Author

KARLA F. C. HOLLOWAY is Associate Professor of English at North Carolina State University and is the Associate Editor of *Obsidian II: Black Literature in Review*. She has contributed articles and essays to the *Journal of Psycholinguistic Research*, *Women and Politics*, and *Women as Elders: The Feminist Politics of Aging*, and is the co-author of *New Dimensions of Spirituality: A Bi-Racial Reading of the Novels of Toni Morrison*.